23

Nelson

English

Developing Fiction Skills

3
BOOK THREE

John Jackman   Wendy Wren

Nelson

Contents

Nuclear Disaster!

Ann Burden is sixteen. Following a nuclear explosion, she believes she is the last person alive on Earth.

May 20th

I am afraid.

Someone is coming.

That is, I think someone is coming, though I am not sure, and I pray that I am wrong. I went into the church and prayed all this morning. I sprinkled water in front of the altar, and put some flowers on it, violets and dogwood.

But there is smoke. For three days there has been smoke, not like the time before. That time, last year, it rose in a great cloud a long way away, and stayed in the sky for two weeks. A forest fire in the dead woods, and then it rained and the smoke stopped. But this time it is a thin column, like a pole, not very high.

And the column has come three times, each time in the late afternoon. At night I cannot see it, and in the morning it is gone. But each afternoon it comes again, and it is nearer. At first it was behind Claypole Ridge, and I could see only the top of it, the smallest smudge. I thought it was a cloud, except that it was too grey, the wrong colour, and then I thought: there are no clouds anywhere else. I got the binoculars and saw that it was narrow and straight; it was smoke from a small fire. When we used to go in the truck, Claypole Ridge was fifteen miles, though it looks closer, and the smoke was coming from behind that.

Beyond Claypole Ridge there is Ogdentown, about ten miles further. But there is no one left alive in Ogdentown.

I know, because after the war ended, and all the telephones went dead, my father, my brother Joseph and cousin David went in the truck to find out what was happening, and the first place they went was Ogdentown. They went early in the morning; Joseph and David were really excited, but Father looked serious.

When they came back it was dark. Mother had been worrying – they took so long – so we were glad to see the truck lights finally coming over Burden Hill, six miles away. They looked like beacons. They were the only lights anywhere, except in the house – no other cars had come down all day. We knew it was the truck because one of the lights, the left one, always blinked when it went over a bump. It came up to the house and they got out; the boys weren't excited any more. They looked scared, and my father looked sick. Maybe he was beginning to be sick, but mainly I think he was distressed.

My mother looked up at him as he climbed down.

"What did you find?"

He said, "Bodies. Just dead bodies. They're all dead."

"All?"

We went inside the house where the lamps were lit, the two boys following, not saying anything. My father sat down. "Terrible," he said, and again, "terrible, terrible. We drove around, looking. We blew the horn. Then we went to the church and rang the bell. You can hear it five miles away. We waited for two hours, but nobody came. I went into a couple of houses – the Johnsons', the Peters' – they were all in there, all dead. There were dead birds all over the streets."

My brother Joseph began to cry. He was fourteen. I think I had not heard him cry for six years.

from *Z for Zachariah* by Robert O'Brien

 ## Comprehension

A **1** In your own words, describe the differences between the smoke Ann sees now and the smoke 'the time before'.

2 How far away was Claypole Ridge?

3 When Ann and her mother saw the lights come over Burden Hill, why were they sure it was their truck?

4 What had Ann's father found in Ogdentown?

B **1** Why does Ann think that 'someone is coming'?

2 Why do you think she is afraid?

3 What do you think has happened to Ann's family?

4 Why do you think the people in Ogdentown are dead, there are 'dead birds all over the streets' and Ann writes about 'dead woods'?

C The first two sentences are unusual for a story opening.

1 How is the writer trying to make you feel?

2 Do you think this is a good opening for a story? Give reasons for your answer.

Vocabulary

Idioms

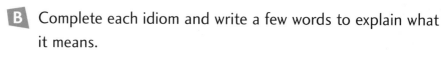
Idioms are short phrases which usually mean something quite different from what you might expect. For example:

I think I'll <u>throw in the towel</u>.

The idiom 'throw in the towel' means 'give up'.

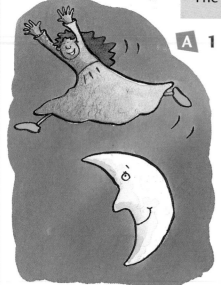

A 1 Copy the two lists below and draw a line to match each idiom to the correct meaning.

a	over the moon	a gloomy person
b	let your hair down	get into trouble
c	a wet blanket	wise for his or her age
d	bring the house down	delighted
e	get into hot water	relax and have fun
f	an old head on young shoulders	cause great amusement

2 Use each idiom from question 1 in a sentence of your own.

B Complete each idiom and write a few words to explain what it means.

1 hit the nail on the _____

2 put your best foot _____

3 get on like a house on _____

4 blow your own _____

5 see things through rose-coloured _____

6 paint the town _____

Spelling

Spelling pattern 'exc'

A common letter pattern at the beginning of words is '**exc**'.

For example:

> The boys weren't <u>exc</u>ited any more.

It is easy to confuse 'exc' words with 'ex' words like '<u>ex</u>act'.

A Write the headings 'exc' and 'ex'. Use a dictionary to help you decide which is the correct spelling of each word below, then write each word under the correct heading.

1	example	excample	**2**	exeed	exceed
3	exercise	excercise	**4**	expert	excpert
5	exel	excel	**6**	exellent	excellent
7	exept	except	**8**	exess	excess
9	expedition	excpedition	**10**	extra	exctra

B **1** What do the 'exc' words you wrote in part A have in common? (There are three things.)

2 Look at the 'exc' words in the box below. What two things make them different from the 'exc' words in part A?

excavate	excuse	exclaim	exclude	exchange

Grammar

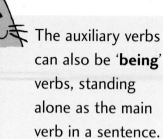

'Being' verbs

The auxiliary verbs can also be '**being**' verbs, standing alone as the main verb in a sentence. For example:
I <u>was</u> angry.

Remember, you sometimes need more than one verb to make a sentence work properly. You may need to use a 'helper' verb, also called an **auxiliary verb**, to help the main verb. The auxiliary verb indicates the tense of the main verb. It tells us whether it happened in the past, the present or the future. For example:
Someone <u>is</u> <u>coming</u>.

| auxiliary verb | main verb |

We use 'is' and 'was' when the sentence is about one person, place or thing. For example:
Father <u>is</u> sick.   He <u>was</u> afraid.

We use 'are' and 'were' with 'you', whether it is singular or plural, or when the sentence is about more than one person, place or thing. For example:
You <u>are</u> afraid.   They <u>are</u> sick.   They <u>were</u> afraid.

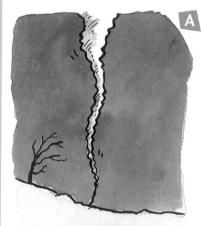

A Copy each sentence and fill the gap with the auxiliary verb 'was' or 'were'.

1 The smoke _____ coming from behind Claypole Ridge.

2 They went in the truck to see what _____ happening.

3 One of the lights on the truck _____ blinking.

4 Father _____ looking sick.

5 The two boys _____ not saying anything.

B Copy each sentence. Add the 'being' verb 'is', 'was', 'are' or 'were'.

1 Until she saw the smoke, Ann thought there _____ nobody else alive.

2 There _____ dead birds all over the streets in Ogdentown.

3 There _____ always a risk of nuclear war if countries keep nuclear weapons.

4 There _____ some countries, including Britain, that still have nuclear bombs.

Sentence construction

Verb tenses

We usually use 'shall' with 'I' and 'we', and 'will' with 'you', 'they', 'he', 'she' and 'it'.

Remember, an **auxiliary verb** is sometimes needed to indicate the **tense** of the main verb. For example:

Verb family name	Past tense	Present tense	Future tense
to look	I looked	I look	I <u>shall</u> look
	I <u>was</u> looking	I <u>am</u> looking	

auxiliary verb

A Copy and complete the table below.

Verb family name	Past tense	Present tense	Future tense
to talk	she <u>talked</u> she _____ talking	she <u>talks</u> she _____ talking	she <u>will</u> <u>talk</u>
to run	I _____ I _____ _____	I _____ I _____ _____	I _____ _____
to see	they _____ they _____ _____	they _____ they _____ _____	they _____ _____
to bring	you _____ you _____ _____	you _____ you _____ _____	you _____ _____

B Write each of these sentences twice, first in the past tense and then in the future tense.

1 The sky looks dark.

2 They drive along the track.

3 We are going home.

Writing

Story openings

Stories for young children usually have a straightforward **opening** which very quickly lets the reader know about the characters and setting in the story. The story then moves through the plot in the order that the events happened.

Stories for older children are not always this straightforward. They may:

- begin in the middle of the plot, and the writer uses 'flashbacks' (descriptions of earlier events) or the thoughts of a character to let you know what happened before
- not describe a character's appearance and personality but let the reader find out more about the character through what he/she says and does.

These story openings really grab your attention and make you want to read more!

Look at the story plot in the boxes below and opposite.

Write the story of Steve's experience of the hurricane. You should:

- write in the first person, as if you are Steve
- begin writing at the point in the story marked ★
- find some way to let the reader know what happened before you went into the cellar
- explain how you felt and what you thought about at each stage of the story.

1 Saturday evening – Steve, who lives alone, makes a cup of coffee.

2 He settles down to watch a quiz on TV.

3 As he watches TV, the wind gets stronger and stronger.

4 The TV programme is interrupted by an announcement that there is a hurricane on the way and people should go to cellars and basements for safety.

5 Steve fetches a torch, biscuits and water, and goes down to the cellar.

6 As the hurricane rages, Steve hears crashes and breaking glass. ⭐

7 The next morning, the hurricane has passed. Steve emerges from the cellar to find destruction everywhere.

The Old Forest

Frodo, Pippin, Sam and Merry have been sent on a long, dangerous journey by the wizard Gandalf. In this part of their journey they are going through the Old Forest, a dark, forbidding and mysterious place.

They picked a way among the trees, and their ponies plodded along, carefully avoiding the many writhing and interlacing roots. There was no undergrowth. The ground was rising steadily, and as they went forward it seemed that the trees became taller, darker, and thicker. There was no sound, except an occasional drip of moisture falling through the still leaves. For the moment there was no whispering or movement among the branches; but they all got an uncomfortable feeling that they were being watched with disapproval … The feeling steadily grew, until they found themselves looking up quickly, or glancing back over their shoulders, as if they expected a sudden blow.

There was not as yet any sign of a path, and the trees seemed constantly to bar their way. Pippin suddenly felt that he could not bear it any longer, and without warning let out a shout. 'Oi! Oi!' he cried. 'I am not going to do anything. Just let me pass through, will you!'

The others halted startled; but the cry fell as if muffled by a heavy curtain. There was no echo or answer though the wood seemed to become more crowded and wakeful than before.

'I should not shout if I were you.' said Merry. 'It does more harm than good.'

Frodo began to wonder if it were possible to find a way through, and if he had been right to make the others come into this abominable wood. Merry was looking from side to side, and seemed already uncertain which way to go. Pippin noticed it. 'It has not taken you long to lose us,' he said. But at that moment Merry gave a whistle of relief and pointed ahead.

'Well, well!' he said. 'These trees do shift. There is the Bonfire Glade in front of us (or I hope so) but the path to it seems to have moved away.'

from The Lord of the Rings by J R R Tolkein

GLOSSARY
writhing twisting
interlacing mixed together, tangled
abominable very unpleasant

Comprehension

A 1 How were Frodo and his friends travelling through the forest?

2 What was the only sound to be heard?

3 What 'feeling' did Frodo and his friends have as they went through the forest?

4 Find the words in the passage which mean the same as:

    a keeping away from

    b happening now and then

    c all the time.

B 1 Do you think Frodo and his friends enjoyed travelling through the wood?

2 Why do you think the writer calls it an 'abominable wood'?

3 How does the description of the forest make you feel?

4 Explain what the writer means when he says that Pippin's cry 'fell as if muffled by a heavy curtain'.

5 How can you tell that Merry was supposed to be guiding the group through the wood?

C We can tell how Frodo, Merry and Pippin are reacting to being in the forest by what they say and do. Write a few sentences about each character, describing what he says and does and what this tells you about him.

Vocabulary

Root words, prefixes and suffixes

Remember, a **root word** is a basic word to which **prefixes** and **suffixes** can be added to make other words from the same word family.
For example:

Root word: comfort

comfort   <u>uncomfort</u><u>able</u>   <u>dis</u>comfort   comfort<u>able</u>

comfort<u>ing</u>   comfort<u>ed</u>   comfort<u>ably</u>   comfort<u>er</u>

A **1** Copy each word below and underline its root word. Then use a dictionary to find out whether the word was originally related to a word from another language.

    a *avoiding*   **b** *dangerous*   **c** *writhing*

    d *interlacing*   **e** *occasional*   **f** *disapproval*

2 Write two more words from the same family as each word in question 1.

Useful prefixes:	**Useful suffixes:**
un dis mis de re al	ly ful ed ing est er al ment ness

B **1** Write three sentences, each using a different word that has the root word 'arrange'.

2 Draw a word web for each root word below, adding all the words you can think of from the same word family.

    a

```
_____              _____
           \            /
            ( certain )
           /            \
_____              _____
```

    b *mystery*   **c** *agree*   **d** *understand*

Spelling

Prefixes

Remember, **prefixes** are groups of letters that can be added at the beginning of a word. Remembering common prefixes can help to improve your spelling.

Below is a table of some frequently used prefixes, with their meanings. Some prefixes have more than one meaning.

Prefix	Meaning	Examples
anti	against	anticlockwise
dis	reverse, remove, separate	dismount
ex	out of	export
fore	previous	foresee
im/in	into	import, intrude
im/in	not	impossible, incapable
mis	badly, wrongly	misbehave
sub	under	subway

A Copy the table of common prefixes (above). Add at least two more examples for each prefix.

B Make up a sentence containing as many words as possible that have prefixes. For example:

Tina <u>dis</u>mounted to <u>re</u>place the wheel of her <u>bi</u>cycle but <u>dis</u>covered that it was <u>im</u>possible to turn the screws <u>anti</u>clockwise, so she had to <u>re</u>turn home on foot.

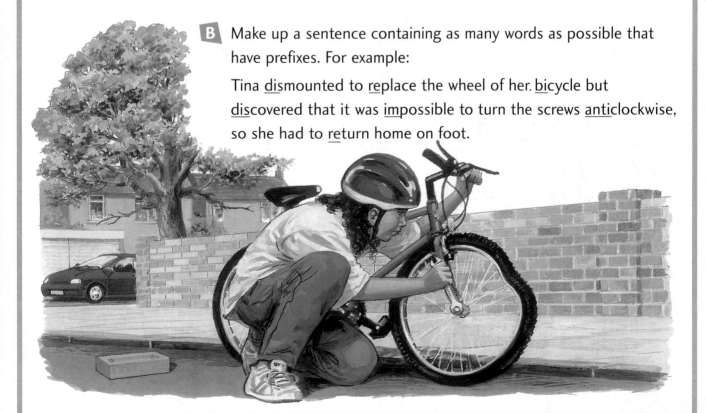

Grammar

Word order

The words and phrases in a sentence can often be arranged in a different **order** that still makes sense. For example:

Homeward the weary ponies plod their way.

The weary ponies plod their way homeward.

The example above still means the same after it has been rearranged. Sometimes, rearranging the words can change the meaning of a sentence. For example:

Before he had gone to sleep, the baby had drunk his milk.

The baby had gone to sleep before he had drunk his milk.

A How many different ways can you find to arrange the words below to make a sentence? You must use all twelve words each time, but the sentences need not all mean the same thing. You may need to add a word or slightly change a word in some versions.

The mysterious wood is certainly a very strange place, the traveller thought.

B Choose a sentence from the passage on page 12. How many different ways can you write the words and phrases so that they still make sense? You may need to change one or two of the words.

Sentence construction

Subject and verb

The **subject** of a sentence is the person, place or thing the sentence is about. Every sentence has to have a **verb**. The subject of the sentence is the person or thing that is doing the action of the verb. For example:

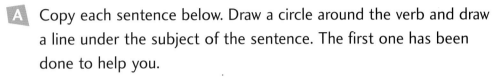

Pippin noticed it.

subject   verb

A Copy each sentence below. Draw a circle around the verb and draw a line under the subject of the sentence. The first one has been done to help you.

1 The ponies (plodded) along.

2 The trees grew taller, darker and thicker.

3 They looked up quickly.

4 Pippin felt he couldn't bear it any longer.

5 The others halted, startled.

6 Merry looked from side to side.

B Copy these sentences, choosing the correct words to fill the gaps.

1 The subject is usually near the beginning/end of the sentence.

2 The verb usually comes before/after the subject.

3 The subject is usually a noun/verb or an adjective/a pronoun.

4 The verb/subject of the sentence usually carries out the action or has the action done to it.

Writing

Characters

A writer tells readers about the **characters** in a story by:
- describing them directly
- letting readers learn about each character through what he or she says and does
- showing the relationship that character has with other characters.

A Look at the passage on page 12. Imagine Frodo and his friends have found their way out of the terrible forest. Write the next part of the story, describing what they do and say in a way that will show the reader that the characters are relieved to have escaped.

B 1 Write a description of a postal worker who delivers letters. Describe:
- what she/he looks like
- what sort of person she/he is. You must decide if she/he is cheerful, bad-tempered, serious and so on.

SORTING OFFICE

2 The postal worker now delivers a parcel to a house, knocking on the door very early in the morning. Let the reader know what sort of person opens the door by what he/she says and does. Write a conversation between the postal worker and the person who opens the door.

a First, plan your writing. You need to:
- Write notes on:
  - the postal worker
  - the person who opens the door
  - their conversation.
- Think about how many paragraphs you will need. For example:

  Paragraph 1 – description of the postal worker

  Paragraph 2 – the postal worker arriving at the door and knocking

  Paragraph 3 – the person opening the door and talking to the postal worker

  Paragraph 4 – the postal worker leaving.

  This paragraph plan is just a suggestion. You may have your own ideas.

b Write your first draft.

c Read through your first draft and think carefully about the words you have used. Do they tell the reader what the characters are like?

Use a thesaurus to help you find more interesting words. Check for any spelling and punctuation mistakes.

d Neatly write your final copy.

Centaurus I

Below is an extract from a play called *Centaurus I* by Jack Richards and James Feldman.

> **Cast**
> NARRATOR 1: also plays MR SOTELO
> NARRATOR 2: also plays VOICE ON TAPE
> GRANT CARTER: Crew member
> MICHELLE CARTER: Crew member
> DON CHAN: Crew member; also plays MR CHAN
> MARGARET CHAN: Crew member
> JOHN FERMI: Captain
> PAULINE SOTELO: Crew member
> PETER BIBIKOV: Executive Officer; also plays MR BIBIKOV

NARRATOR 1:   In the year 2000, the spaceship *Centaurus I* left Earth and headed for its nearest galactic neighbour, Centaurus Proxima. Problems on Earth had grown so great that many people doubted man's ability to survive. *Centaurus I* is provided with all things needed to educate, feed, and entertain a crew numbering 100. The present generation – the 17th – has lost identification with its ancestors, as well as with the original purpose of the trip.
To the people aboard, the ship has become their world. The closer they come to their destination, the more unbearable becomes the thought of giving up their security for an alien life.

NARRATOR 2:   It is now October, 2492. You are on the earthship *Centaurus I*, which is 492 years away from Earth on its journey to the solar system of Centaurus Proxima. As the play opens, some members of the crew are involved in a serious conversation.

GRANT: *(Loudly)* I've said it again and again. We must go back before it's too late.

MICHELLE: We'll never turn back as long as Captain Fermi is in command.

DON: I agree. He's impossible to reason with.

GRANT: Then we'll not try to reason with him. We'll use force to take the ship from him. Don't you know that tomorrow we reach PNR?

MARGARET: What do you mean, PNR?

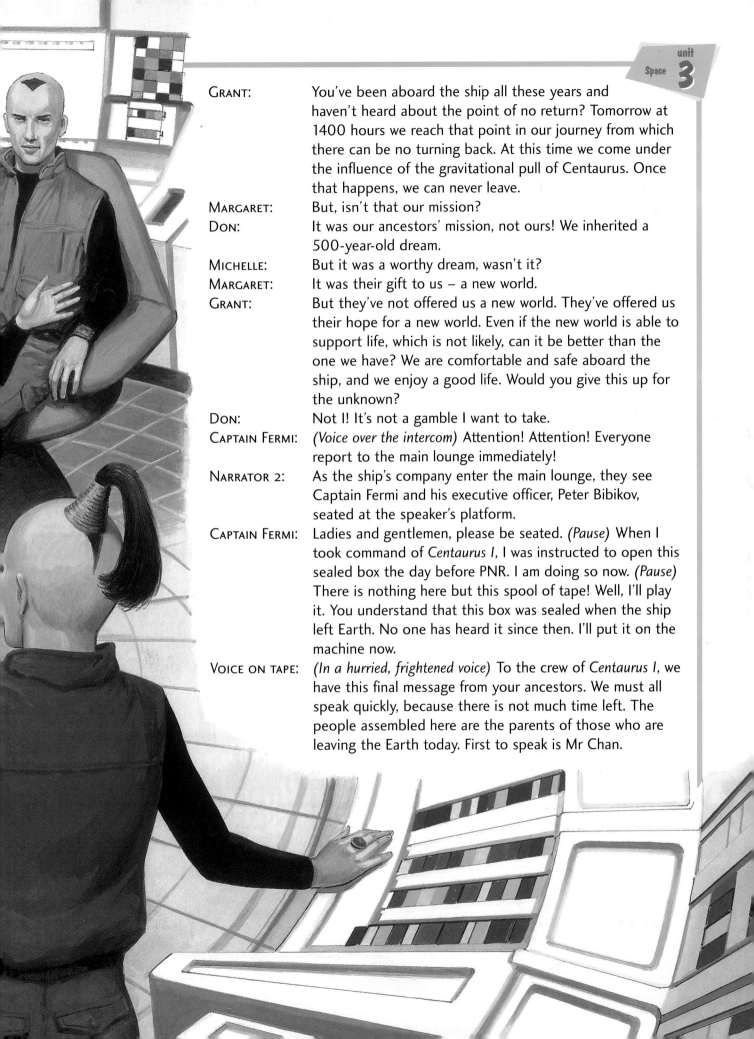

GRANT:	You've been aboard the ship all these years and haven't heard about the point of no return? Tomorrow at 1400 hours we reach that point in our journey from which there can be no turning back. At this time we come under the influence of the gravitational pull of Centaurus. Once that happens, we can never leave.
MARGARET:	But, isn't that our mission?
DON:	It was our ancestors' mission, not ours! We inherited a 500-year-old dream.
MICHELLE:	But it was a worthy dream, wasn't it?
MARGARET:	It was their gift to us – a new world.
GRANT:	But they've not offered us a new world. They've offered us their hope for a new world. Even if the new world is able to support life, which is not likely, can it be better than the one we have? We are comfortable and safe aboard the ship, and we enjoy a good life. Would you give this up for the unknown?
DON:	Not I! It's not a gamble I want to take.
CAPTAIN FERMI:	*(Voice over the intercom)* Attention! Attention! Everyone report to the main lounge immediately!
NARRATOR 2:	As the ship's company enter the main lounge, they see Captain Fermi and his executive officer, Peter Bibikov, seated at the speaker's platform.
CAPTAIN FERMI:	Ladies and gentlemen, please be seated. *(Pause)* When I took command of *Centaurus I*, I was instructed to open this sealed box the day before PNR. I am doing so now. *(Pause)* There is nothing here but this spool of tape! Well, I'll play it. You understand that this box was sealed when the ship left Earth. No one has heard it since then. I'll put it on the machine now.
VOICE ON TAPE:	*(In a hurried, frightened voice)* To the crew of *Centaurus I*, we have this final message from your ancestors. We must all speak quickly, because there is not much time left. The people assembled here are the parents of those who are leaving the Earth today. First to speak is Mr Chan.

MR CHAN:	I am sending my son and my name into space because neither will continue here on Earth. Oh, please keep us alive on your new planet! Here we are starving. The world is overflowing with people. There is no room left to grow food. And that which we grow is taken from us by wild bands of starving humanity. Please, please keep life going!
MR BIBIKOV:	*(Hoarsely)* I am Dimitri Bibikov. As my son boards the ship, I can think only that he will breathe clean air for the first time in his life. Our planet is covered with black smoke. Our lives are a constant struggle against the filthy air. Our lungs are ruined. We are sick. May you find, wherever you go, air that will give you life, not hurry your death …
CAPTAIN:	*(Shouting)* All aboard! Quickly!
MR SOTELO:	*(Shouting)* We are the last Sotelos on Earth! The Earth is finished! Life is over! Go quickly!
VOICE ON TAPE:	*(Speaking hurriedly, but softly)* The Captain is waiting for this spool of tape. Ladies and gentlemen of the future, think of what you have just heard. You are being sent to keep mankind alive somewhere in the universe. When you hear this tape, you will be faced with the same awesome responsibility we are faced with today – to decide the fate of your descendants. May wisdom guide your thinking. Good-bye. Bless you. Good-bye from Earth.

 Comprehension

A 1   How many were in the crew of *Centaurus I*?
   2   When did it leave Earth?
   3   Who is in command in October 2492?
   4   What does PNR stand for?

B Explain the following phrases in your own words.

   1   impossible to reason with
   2   We inherited a 500-year-old dream
   3   starving humanity
   4   awesome responsibility

C Explain what you think is the purpose of the two narrators.

Vocabulary

Synonyms for 'said'

The careful selection of expressive words adds to the quality of your writing. Here is a list of some of the many words which are **synonyms** for 'said':

> warned stated asked retorted answered shouted
> stammered objected inquired sobbed laughed observed
> cried growled remarked urged gabbled replied
> interrupted whimpered roared grumbled mumbled
> muttered drawled commented whispered explained
> exclaimed continued pleaded called agreed

A Copy each sentence, choosing the best word from the box above to replace 'said'.

1 "We must go back before it's too late," said Grant.

2 "We'll never turn back as long as Captain Fermi is in command," said Michelle.

3 "Yes, he's impossible to reason with," said Don.

4 "What do you mean, PNR?" said Margaret.

5 "Tomorrow we reach the point in our journey from which there can be no turning back," said Grant.

6 "It was our ancestors' mission, not ours!" said Don.

7 "The Earth is finished! Life is over!" said Mr Sotelo.

8 "Surely they wouldn't blow up their planet!" said Don.

9 "Enough of this! How many want to turn back?" said Grant.

B Make up three more pieces of dialogue that might have been spoken by members of the crew. Don't use 'said' or any of the synonyms for 'said' that you've used so far.

Spelling

Suffixes – 'ous' and 'ious'

The **suffixes** '**ous**' and '**ious**' are quite common and are usually added to words that end with 'or' or 'our'. When adding 'ous' or 'ious' to most words ending with 'our', first remove the 'u' from the word to which the suffix is being added. For example:

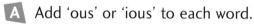

vap<u>o</u>ur   vap<u>orous</u>   censor   censor<u>ious</u>

A Add 'ous' or 'ious' to each word.

Use a dictionary if you need to check the definitions.

1 *rigour*   2 *labour*   3 *vigour*   4 *humour*   5 *glamour*

B Use each of the new words that you formed in part A in a sentence of your own.

Grammar

Direct and reported speech

Direct speech is when you write the exact words that a person said. We show this by putting speech marks (" ") around the spoken words. For example:

   "What do you mean, PNR?" asked Margaret.

Reported speech or **indirect speech** is when you write about (or report) what a person has said, without using the actual words spoken, so you don't need speech marks. For example:

   Margaret asked what he meant by PNR.

Speech marks are also called inverted commas.

A Write each of these sentences as reported speech.

1   *"What happens when we run short of fuel?" asked Don anxiously.*

2   *"That simply isn't possible," replied Captain Fermi.*

3   *"What a ridiculous claim," shouted Grant, leaping to his feet.*

4   *"I am in charge of this craft," warned the Captain, "so treat me with respect."*

B Write each of these sentences as direct speech.

1 Michelle told Margaret that she thought Grant had said too much.

2 Don grabbed Grant's arm and begged him to sit down.

3 Grant muttered to Don that time was running out.

4 Don tried to persuade him that it was safer to go on than to return to Earth.

 **Sentence construction**

Direct speech

Remember, you need to use inverted commas when writing **direct speech**. You also have to use correct punctuation and start a new line whenever a different person speaks. For example:

"We must go back before it's too late," said Grant in a loud voice.

"We'll never turn back as long as Captain Fermi is in command," commented Michelle.

A Choose a few lines from the playscript on pages 20–22 and convert them into direct speech, using speech marks, commas and new lines whenever they are needed.

B Write an imaginary conversation between you and a friend about whether you would like to visit another planet and, if so, which one.

Writing

Playscripts

Writing a play is different from writing a story, because the audience is not reading it but watching or listening as it is acted out. However, a **playscript** still needs:

- plot
- setting
- characters.

A playwright usually indicates the setting of each scene, then writes the words that each character says, and adds stage directions to tell the actors what to do and how to say their lines.

Below is a table, briefly showing how the passengers aboard the *Centaurus I* react to the tape that Captain Fermi plays to them.

Character	What he/she thinks
Captain Fermi	insists they continue the journey doesn't give reasons expects to be obeyed because he is captain
Grant	doesn't think that what they have heard makes any difference wants to turn back
Pauline	calm and reasonable thinks they should respect what their ancestors say and gives reasons, such as: the Earth is finished and to go back would give humans 500 years more of life, but to go on would bring the chance of finding a planet where the human race could exist for much longer
Don	does not want to go beyond PNR
Michelle	doesn't think anyone is left on Earth because no one has answered their messages thinks something awful has happened on Earth
Margaret	very uncertain and confused wants to take a vote on what to do

Use the information in the table to write the next scene of *Centaurus I*. The setting is the same as in the first scene and the characters should discuss what they heard on the tape and come to a decision about whether to turn back or go on.

Use stage directions to tell the actors:

- how to behave
- how to say their lines.

Set out your playscript with the characters' names on the left and the dialogue on the right. Use brackets to show the stage directions. For example:

GRANT: (*Loudly*) I've said it again and again.

Visiting London

Trip to London

By seven o'clock we were on our way
by train to London for the day,
four hours of travelling in the sun,
arrived in rain at Paddington
with neighbours, friends, mother and me,
and everyone had come to see
the big shops and the well-known sights,
the famous streets with all their lights.

We strolled together everywhere,
fed pigeons in Trafalgar Square
who did not mind the drizzle there,
watched snorting traffic whizzing by,
waved at old Nelson standing high,
then sloshed our way to Waterloo
and, after lunch, went to the Zoo;
we managed to spend half an hour
learning history at the Tower
and just had time to see Hyde Park,
Buckingham Palace through the dark,
and going back I fell asleep
having no need for counting sheep.

We got back home at half-past eleven
and glad I was but still thanked heaven
for all I'd done and all I'd seen
though wished that I had met the Queen,
but never once shall I forget
slopping round London in the wet,
glad to be back with country things,
the trees and hills and murmurings
of bees in fields, birds on trees,
and rambling free and at my ease
whether in sun or whirling snow,
and all the people whom I know.

by Leonard Clark

Comprehension

A 1 What impression does the poet give you of London?

2 Do you think he prefers London or the countryside?

3 The verses in the poem are of different lengths. Why do you think the poet split the poem where he did?

Hint: What is each verse about?

4 The rhythm the poet has used means that you can read the poem quickly. What impression does this give you of the trip to London?

Changing Times

Many things are changing
Today in London Town
New buildings going up
Old ones coming down
Just like London people
Houses too grow old
And can no longer do their job
To keep out damp and cold
Many are old fashioned
And were built long ago
For people in a different age
Who didn't hurry so
People's ways are changing
Like the things we use
Telephones for speaking
Television news

Just try to imagine
How things used to be
Different songs to listen to
Different things to see
Everyone used horses
Or else their own two feet
Everything moved slowly
Like the policeman on his beat
No motor cars to take them
Quickly on their way
No discos or videos
Like there are today
No package holidays
And no aeroplanes
No electric railways
And only puffer trains
People used to manage
It didn't matter how
But when you come to think of it
Aren't you glad it's NOW.

by Eric Slayter

unit
London
4

Comprehension

B Make a list of the words and phrases that would make sense in each of the gaps in the paragraph below. Draw a neat line under the word in each list that you would choose to use.

Towns and cities have changed ___1___ in the last 100 years. It is now ___2___ easier for people to ___3___ to work using ___4___ , which means they can ___5___ farther away. Also, travel by ___6___ has meant that some people can take holidays in ___7___ places. Some forms of entertainment that are popular today, such as ___8___ , weren't even invented in the 1800s.

C Copy and complete this table.

Poem	Number of verses	Rhyming pattern	3 pairs of rhyming words
Trip to London			way/day / /
Changing Times			/ / /

Vocabulary

Adverbs in dialogue

Remember, when you write conversations using **direct speech** (the exact words people said, inside speech marks), it is called **dialogue**.

Remember, **adverbs** tell us more about verbs. They usually tell us how, when or where actions happen. They are helpful in dialogue (speech) because they give information about how words are spoken.

For example:

"Are we nearly there?" asked the boy, <u>wearily</u>.

| verb | adverb |

The adverb 'wearily' tells us more about the verb 'asked'.

A Choose an adverb from the box, or think of one of your own, to complete each sentence.

| *irritably   quietly   anxiously   cheerfully* |

1 "Keep close to me or you'll get lost," Mum said _____ .
2 "Want to buy some pigeon food?" asked the man _____ .
3 "Hurry along!" the bus conductor _____ shouted.
4 "Can we visit the Tower of London?" I whispered to Mum _____ .

B 1 Make a list of adverbs that end with 'ly' that you might use in dialogue.
2 Think back to a long or boring journey you have been on. Write four dialogue sentences, each including an adverb, that you or others who were with you might have spoken. For example:

"Why is the train so late?" Monica <u>angrily</u> demanded.

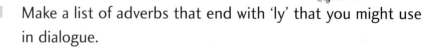

Spelling

Suffixes

To add a **suffix** to a word that ends with 'e', you need to remove the 'e' if the suffix begins with a vowel. For example:

wak<u>e</u> + '<u>i</u>ng' = waking

If the suffix begins with a consonant, you can keep the 'e'. For example:

wak<u>e</u> + '<u>f</u>ul' = wakeful

Most spelling rules have exceptions! You need to remove the 'e' from the end of the following words, even if the suffix begins with a consonant:

true truly   argue argument   due duly

A Write the new word that is formed when you add the suffix to each word below.

1 argue + 'ing'   2 place + 'ed'   3 state + 'ment'

4 package + 'ing'   5 combine + 'ation'   6 safe + 'ty'

7 relate + 'ion'   8 shame + 'ful'   9 imagine + 'ation'

10 insure + 'ance'   11 care + 'less'   12 share + 'ing'

B Make a list of five verbs that end with 'e'. To each one, add as many suffixes as you can to make other words from the same word family.

Grammar

Slang

In most parts of the country, people use words and phrases that are not Standard English. This is known as **slang**. In London, some people use what is called **rhyming slang**. For example:

'apples and <u>pears</u>' is rhyming slang for '<u>stairs</u>'

It is called rhyming slang because the last word of the slang phrase rhymes with the word it stands for, for example:

'mince <u>pies</u>' for '<u>eyes</u>'

A What do you think each of these rhyming slang phrases might mean? The clues will help you.

1 little Bo Peep (something we do at night)

2 plates of meat (we stand on these)

3 boat race (this is on the front of your head)

4 dog and bone (we talk to each other using one of these)

5 pen and ink (unpleasant smell)

Slang words are often used when speaking but are not normally used in writing.

Dictionaries usually include slang words, so look up any you are unsure about.

B 1 Write two non-slang synonyms for each of the underlined words below.

  a She told a <u>whopper</u>.   b He <u>belted</u> around the corner.
  c He was <u>broke</u>.   d I <u>bashed</u> my arm on the door.
  e Use your <u>loaf</u>.   f Don't be so <u>stingy</u>.

  2 Write four slang words or phrases and then write each in another way, using Standard English.

 ## Sentence construction

Using the past tense

When recounting (telling of things you have done or seen), you need to use the **past tense**. For example:

  Everything <u>moved</u> slowly.

A Write these future-tense sentences in the past tense, as though you were writing to a friend about a trip to London. Underline the words you had to change. The first one has been done to help you.

1 *We are going to London to see some of the famous sights.*

  We <u>went</u> to London to see some of the famous sights.

2 *We will be travelling by coach to Victoria.*

3 *I will enjoy having a day off school!*

4 *We will be taking packed lunches.*

5 *My bag might be too heavy, as I am taking lots of things with me.*

6 *We will have a great time, whatever the weather is like.*

B Write five or six sentences in the past tense, recounting something you have enjoyed doing in the last few days.

Writing

Contrast

Writers often show how they feel about their subject by **contrasting** things – comparing them and showing their differences.

Most of the poem 'A Trip to London' is about sightseeing in the city, but the last verse contrasts London with the poet's everyday life in the country.

In 'Changing Times', the poet contrasts London today with how it used to be.

Write a poem called 'A Trip to the Beach'. Your poem should have two verses.

- The first verse should describe a crowded beach in summer.
- The second verse should describe a deserted beach in winter.

Make sure the reader knows which you prefer by the words you use.

You could begin your poem like this:

> By seven o'clock we were on our way
> by train to the seaside for the day.

The Flight of Icarus

This Ancient Greek myth tells the story of Daedalus, a great engineer and inventor, and his son, Icarus, who were held captive by the King of Crete on his island.

The king gave Daedalus a well-equipped workshop in a high tower, but even this was not sufficient to make the inventor content to remain in Crete. He wanted the freedom to leave the island and return to his own country. Realising this, the King ordered that all ships should be searched before leaving port, to check that Daedalus and Icarus had not hidden themselves on board.

But the two were determined to leave, and if they could not escape by sea they would find another way! From his tower, Daedalus watched the birds and an idea suddenly came to him. He would build Icarus and himself a set of wings each! He sent Icarus to collect all the feathers he could find and soon the workshop was full of thousands of them. Next, Daedalus made a wooden frame shaped like the wing of a bird. He poured melted wax onto the frame, and into the wax he pressed the feathers. Then he let the wax cool and become solid again. To his delight, when he attached the wings to his shoulders, he could feel the wind trying to lift him into the air. Immediately, he set to work to make a pair of wings for Icarus. Daedalus was sure that he and his son could jump from the tower and fly across the sea.

When they were ready to leave, Daedalus gave the boy some advice. "If you fly too low, the spray from the waves will make your wings wet and heavy, and if you fly too high, the heat from the sun will melt the wax that holds the feathers together. Stay near me and you will be safe." With a feeling of great excitement, they climbed onto the window ledge. Daedalus smiled at his son, then jumped. At first the wings did not seem to be lifting him. Desperately he flapped his wings and then, slowly at first, he was carried up into the sky. He glanced over his shoulder to see Icarus close behind.

What a thrill young Icarus felt, to be flying like a bird. With sheer delight, he soared higher and higher, up towards the clouds. Daedalus suddenly realised that Icarus was too excited to remember his father's warning. Up, up, soared the boy, through the clouds – and then above them.

"Icarus, my son, come back! The sun will melt the wax!" pleaded Daedalus, but Icarus was now too far away to hear the cries of his father. Suddenly, Icarus remembered. It was too late! He could see the feathers beginning to come away from the wooden frame – first a few, then more and more. He began to lose height. Faster and faster he fell towards the sea, with the feathers scattering around him as he crashed down past his desperate, helpless father.

Daedalus pulled the boy's limp body from the sea and flew back to land where, weeping bitterly, he buried him. Some time later, Daedalus built a temple to Apollo, the sun god. In it, he hung his wings as an offering to the god. Never again would Daedalus fly.

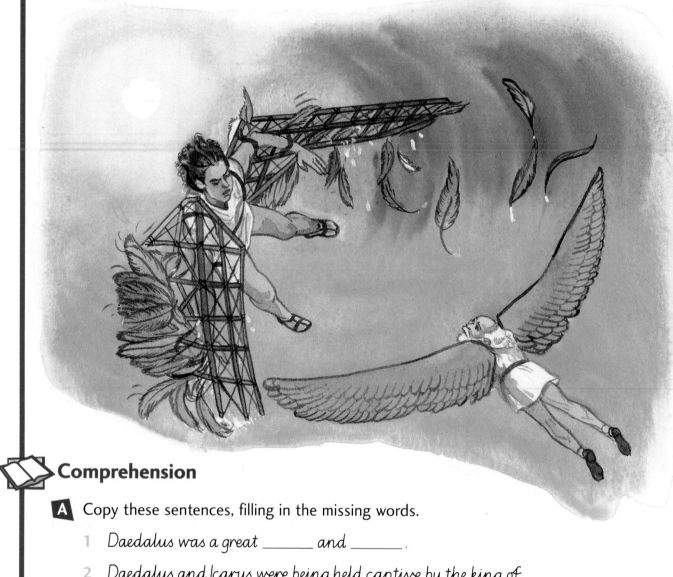

Comprehension

A Copy these sentences, filling in the missing words.

1 Daedalus was a great _____ and _____.

2 Daedalus and Icarus were being held captive by the king of _____.

3 Icarus became too _____ to remember his father's instruction not to fly too high.

4 Daedalus wept _____ as he buried his son's body.

B 1 Why do you think Daedalus wanted to return home?

2 What do you think of Daedalus's idea to fly to freedom?

3 What words describe how Daedalus felt as he watched Icarus falling to his death?

4 Imagine that you could fly like a bird for one day. Make a list of words that you might use to describe the sensations you would experience.

C Make a paragraph plan for the story of Icarus, writing brief notes on what each paragraph is about.

Vocabulary

Prefixes that make antonyms

Remember, **antonyms** are opposites.

Remember, the **antonyms** of some words are made by adding a **prefix**. For example:

sufficient	<u>in</u>sufficient	possible	<u>im</u>possible
wise	<u>un</u>wise	honest	<u>dis</u>honest

A Choose a prefix to make the antonym of each word.

1 happy   2 appear   3 tie   4 trust

5 cover   6 sure   7 capable   8 perfect

B 1 Think of eight more words that can have a prefix added to make their antonym. Write down each word and its antonym.

2 Put three of the antonyms from question 1 into sentences of your own to show their meaning.

Spelling

Homophones

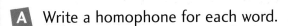

Remember, **homophones** are words that sound the same, but are spelt differently. For example:

Daedalus could <u>see</u> Icarus plunging towards the <u>sea</u>,
and realised that his <u>son</u> had flown too near the <u>sun</u>.

A Write a homophone for each word.

1 allowed   2 alter   3 beech   4 boy

5 fair   6 hair   7 hear   8 hour

9 no   10 plain   11 rain   12 scene

B Write sentences about Icarus and Daedalus, using four of the pairs of homophones from part A.

Grammar

Common and proper nouns

Common nouns are the words we use to name things. For example:
feather

Proper nouns are the 'special' names of people or places. For example:
Apollo

A 1 Write down six common nouns and three proper nouns from the passage on pages 36–37.

2 Copy the following sentence into your book. Underline the common nouns and draw a circle around the proper nouns.

On Monday, our teacher, Miss Robbins, read the class the story of Icarus.

B 1 Look at a book that you have been reading recently. Make a list of ten common nouns and five proper nouns from the book.

2 Write some proper nouns that relate to you, your family and friends, and to where you live.

3 Look straight ahead of you. Write all the common nouns you can see.

Punctuation

Direct speech

Here is part of a conversation that might have taken place between Icarus and his father. When you write dialogue (speech), you need to tell your readers who is speaking, and use speech marks around the words he/she actually says. Remember, when we write the exact words that somebody says, it is called **direct speech**.

"Icarus, I need you to bring me some feathers," said Daedalus.
"Why do you need feathers?" asked his son.
"You ask too many questions," Daedalus replied. "Just do as I ask."
"But where should I look?" enquired Icarus. "I can't simply go and ask the birds, can I?" he added, rudely.

Notice that a new line is started each time a different person starts to speak.

Remember, start a new line each time a different person starts to speak.

A Copy the conversation below, adding the speech marks and other missing punctuation marks.

If you were clever you would not ask such silly questions said Daedalus Look there is a butchers shop across the street Does that give you a clue Yes it does replied the boy I will go and ask them for the feathers from the chickens they have plucked That is more like it said his father Be as quick as you can We dont have much time

B Make up three or four more sentences to finish the conversation from part A. Write them as direct speech.

Writing

Myths and legends

Most cultures have **myths** and **legends** – traditional stories from long ago which tell of heroes and heroines who performed brave deeds and fought against villains and monsters.

In *Developing Fiction Skills Book 1*, you may already have read about how Merlin helped Arthur to become King, and how Theseus killed the dreaded Minotaur.

In the myth of Daedalus and Icarus, Daedalus showed great courage and daring to escape from Crete, but the story ended in tragedy.

A 1 Imagine you are Icarus and it is the night before you are going to attempt to escape using the wings that your father, Daedalus, has made. You find it impossible to sleep. Are you frightened? Excited? Write about your thoughts and feelings as you lie in bed watching the sun rise.

2 Read the story of Daedalus and Icarus again. Rewrite the story using pictures and very simple captions that you could read and share with a younger child.

Greek myths and legends often involve the gods and goddesses whom the Ancient Greeks worshipped. They believed that the gods and goddesses lived on Mount Olympus and sometimes behaved like ordinary people, squabbling amongst themselves and always trying to get the better of one another! Their interference in the affairs of mortals (humans) often caused trouble. Read the story below, which tells how the Trojan War, which lasted ten years, was brought about because of a quarrel among the gods.

Two of the immortals (gods and goddesses), Thetis and Peleus, were getting married and all the gods and goddesses of Mount Olympus were invited to the wedding. All, that is, except one – Eris, the goddess of discord (disagreement). Wherever she was, there was always trouble. Quarrels broke out over the slightest thing and friendly gatherings and celebrations were ruined. Therefore, Eris was not invited to the wedding.

Quite naturally, Eris was furious at being left out. She decided to spoil the wedding for everyone else. As the guests gathered in the hall where the feast was to be held, Eris strode in. To the astonishment of all those assembled, she tossed a golden apple onto the table and left. Looking closely at the apple, the guests could see that there was an inscription carved on it. It read, 'For the fairest'.

Immediately, the goddesses began to argue among themselves as to who was the fairest. The quarrel dragged on and many goddesses withdrew from the contest, but Hera – the queen of the goddesses, Aphrodite – the goddess of love, and Athene – the goddess of war, would not give way. Each was determined that the golden apple should be hers.

Zeus, the King of the gods, was not prepared to be the judge as he feared offending any one of these powerful goddesses. He decided that the decision should be left to a mortal and the choice fell on Paris, King Priam's son.

Zeus called the messenger god, Hermes, and told him to take the three goddesses to where Paris was tending his father's flocks on the slopes of Mount Ida. Paris was extremely surprised at their request and, like Zeus, he did not want to become involved in judging the three goddesses but he had to do as Hermes wished.

Each of the goddesses tried to bribe Paris. Hera promised to make him lord of all Asia. Athene promised that he would always be victorious in battle. Aphrodite promised him the love of the most beautiful woman in the world. It did not take long for Paris to reach his verdict. He gave the golden apple to Aphrodite.

Now, the most beautiful woman in the world was Helen, wife of the Greek lord, Meneleus. True to Aphrodite's promise, Paris carried Helen off to his father's kingdom of Troy. Hera and Aphrodite saw an opportunity to punish Paris for not awarding either of them the golden apple. They helped the Greeks to attack and totally destroy the city of Troy in a war that lasted for ten years.

GLOSSARY
bribe a gift to persuade somebody to do what you want
inscription carved or written message
verdict decision

B In this myth, the quarrel between the three goddesses caused a war among the mortals.
Write your own myth about a quarrel among the gods and goddesses that causes trouble for a mortal character.
You must decide:
- the names of the gods and goddesses
  (you could make up the names, or you could try to find out the names of some more Greek gods and goddesses)
- how the quarrel begins
- which mortal is chosen to sort it out
- how the decision causes more trouble.

A Buddhist Tale

This is a story from the Buddhist faith, which teaches a lesson in an amusing way.

Once upon a time, there lived a king who gathered around him many wise and learned men to advise him. The King, however, soon began to think that these men were not so very wise after all, as they quarrelled constantly and could never agree about anything.

One day, the King ordered the wise men to meet him in front of the palace. Here, on the King's orders, there were gathered all the blind men who lived in the city, and an elephant. Instructing the wise men to pay attention, the King told each of the blind men in turn to describe what the elephant was like.

The first blind man was led to the elephant and put his hands on the tusks. "There is no doubt," he cried. "The elephant is like a carrot!"

The second blind man felt the elephant's ear, declaring the elephant to be just like a fan. When the third blind man touched the elephant's trunk, he backed away in horror shouting, "It's a snake! It's a snake!"

The fourth blind man felt the elephant's leg. "It is obvious that this elephant is like a tree." When the fifth blind man caught hold of the elephant's tail he was absolutely convinced that the elephant was like a rope.

Many other blind men felt the elephant and each had his own idea as to what it was like. Soon, quarrels broke out. Angry words were shouted. One man pushed another. The quarrels turned into fights, as each blind man was sure he was right.

The wise men looked on in amazement at the way the blind men were behaving and some of them even began to laugh.

"Why are you laughing?" enquired the King. "The way these blind men are behaving is no different to how you behave! You are always quarrelling because you cannot see anyone else's point of view. Each of you is so sure you are right and everyone else is wrong. The blind men only felt one part of the elephant. They didn't bother to feel all of it. You only see one side of an argument. You never bother to look at it from all sides and, until you do, you will never understand anything properly."

Comprehension A Read the story carefully and answer the questions.

1 Why did the King gather the blind men together?

2 When the blind men examined the elephant, what mistake did they all make?

3 Find the following words and phrases in the story and write them in your own words.

a quarrelled constantly

b pay attention

c absolutely convinced

d looked on in amazement

4 What was the King trying to prove to the wise men?

5 Do you think this was a good way to prove his point? Give your reasons.

The Blind Men and the Elephant

It was six men of Hindostan,
    To learning much inclined,
Who went to see the elephant,
    (Though all of them were blind):
That each by observation
    Might satisfy his mind.

The *first* approached the Elephant,
    And happening to fall
Against his broad and sturdy side,
    At once began to bawl:
"Bless me, it seems the Elephant
    Is very like a wall."

The *second*, feeling of his tusk,
    Cried, "Ho! what have we here
So very round and smooth and sharp?
    To me 'tis mighty clear
This wonder of an Elephant
    Is very like a spear."

The *third* approached the animal,
    And happening to take
The squirming trunk within his hands,
    Then boldly up and spake:
"I see," quoth he, "the Elephant
    Is very like a snake."

The *fourth* stretched out his eager hand
    And felt about the knee,
"What most this mighty beast is like
    Is mighty plain," quoth he;
" 'Tis clear enough the Elephant
    Is very like a tree."

The *fifth* who chanced to touch the ear
    Said, "Even the blindest man
Can tell what this resembles most;
    Deny the fact who can,
This marvel of an Elephant
    Is very like a fan."

The *sixth* no sooner had begun
    About the beast to grope,
Than, seizing on the swinging tail
    That fell within his scope,
"I see," cried he, "the Elephant
    Is very like a rope."

And so these men of Hindostan
    Disputed loud and long,
Each in his own opinion
    Exceeding stiff and strong,
Though *each* was *partly* in the right
    And *all were in the wrong*.

by John Godfrey Saxe

 Comprehension

B   1   Carefully read the story and the poem again. Make notes on the details that are the same, and the details that are different.

    2   Does the fact that the details in the story differ from those in the poem make any difference to the point they are both trying to make?

    3   Do you think the poem or the story makes the point most strongly? Give your reasons.

GLOSSARY
bawl shout
quoth said
spake said

Vocabulary

Idioms

Idioms are used to describe something by likening it to something else. For example:

'He blew his top.' describes an angry person as if he were an exploding volcano.

'I'm really in a hole.' compares a difficult situation to a deep hole.

A Write what each sentence means.

1 He's in hot water.
2 My hands are tied.
3 We got on like a house on fire.
4 She was really dragging her feet.

B Write sentences which mean the same as these.

1 "You're on the wrong track," said one man.
2 "Don't get on your high horse with me!" snapped another.
3 "Keep your hair on!" replied the first man.
4 The King told them both to pack it in, so they shut up.

Spelling

'ea' and 'oo'
letter patterns

The '**ea**' letter pattern has more than one sound. For example:
   the h<u>ea</u>d of the gr<u>ea</u>t b<u>ea</u>st

A 1 Draw a table like the one below, and finish writing the words from the box in the correct columns. Some words go in more than one column.

> steak   jealous   heater   breakable✓ measure   feather
>   please   read   greatly   meat   weak   lead   beating✓
>   bread   heaven✓ seat   pleasure   head   greater

'ea' sounds like 'eh'	'ea' sounds like 'ai'	'ea' sounds like 'ee'
heaven	breakable	beating

2 a Which words from the box went in more than one column?
  b What do we call words like these?

B 1 Find and copy the words in 'A Buddhist Tale' that have the 'ea' letter pattern. Next to each word you have copied, write two others that have an 'ea' pattern that makes the same sound.

The '**oo**' letter pattern has a different sound in the words 'f<u>oo</u>t' and 'sm<u>oo</u>th'.

2 a Write four words in which the 'oo' sounds the same as in 'foot'.

b Write four words in which the 'oo' sounds the same as in 'smooth'.

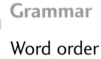

Grammar

Word order

The **order** of words in a sentence can sometimes be changed and still make sense. Sometimes, changing the order of the words gives the sentence a different meaning. Sometimes the meaning stays the same. For example:

- All the blind men were gathered together in front of the palace by the King.
- All the blind men were gathered together by the King in front of the palace.
- All the blind men in front of the palace were gathered together by the King.

A Carefully read the three sentences in the box above and think about how they are different. Explain in your own words what each sentence means.

B Write each of these sentences in a different way.

1 In a few moments the market place was a tangle of fighting bodies.

2 You'll never understand anything properly unless you look at it from different angles.

3 You are always late because you never wear a watch.

49

Sentence construction

Clauses and commas

Sometimes it is good to use short sentences. For example:

> Soon quarrels broke out. Angry words were shouted. One man pushed another.

This helps the reader to get a sense of how quickly things were happening. At other times, it is better to write in longer sentences made up of two or more **clauses**. However, longer sentences need to be broken up into sections, to help them make sense. We use **commas** to split up sentences and tell readers where to make a slight pause. For example:

> The King stood up and, making sure that the wise men were paying attention, he told each of the blind men to describe the elephant.

Remember, a **clause** is a part of a sentence and contains a verb.

A In each of the sentences below, one clause makes sense by itself. Copy each sentence and neatly underline the clause which could be a short sentence by itself.

1 To cut a long story short, each man described the animal in a different way.

2 The wise man looked at all this, amazed and amused.

3 You must learn to examine ideas from every side, as the blind men should have examined the elephant.

B Write another clause or two that you could add to each sentence.

1 The King told them all to stop arguing.

2 Each of the learned men thought he was right.

3 The elephant wondered what was happening.

Writing

Fables

Many traditional or religious stories have been told for hundreds of years, but the details are often different from one version to another.

A Write your own version of the story of the blind men and the elephant, but change the story so that the blind men have a different animal or object to describe. Plan:

* what the animal or object is
* the part of it that each blind man touches
* what each part is mistaken for.

Fables are stories that usually have a **moral** – a message or a lesson for the reader. Many fables are about animals. Many of the fables that we know today were written by a man called Aesop, who lived in Greece about 2,500 years ago. His fables teach lessons that are still useful today.

B Read each fable carefully, then write down what lesson you think it is trying to teach.

A lion was just about to eat a hare that was sleeping in the grass, when he saw a deer run by. The lion left the hare to chase after the deer. The noise of the chase woke the hare. The lion chased the deer for a long time, but he got tired and gave up. He went back to catch the hare, but found that it had run away.

A tortoise wanted an eagle to teach it to fly. The eagle thought that this was a silly idea, as the tortoise had no wings. But the tortoise begged the eagle until he agreed. The eagle gripped the tortoise in his claws, carried him to a great height and let go. The poor tortoise fell onto some rocks and was broken into pieces.

C Write a fable of your own which teaches a lesson. You could use one of the ideas on the left, or one of your own.

Look before you leap.

Once bitten, twice shy.

Things are not always what they seem.

Be kind to others and they will be kind to you.

- Think about the characters you need in the fable. Many of Aesop's fables are about animals that can talk and often act like humans. When animals or objects are shown behaving like human beings, it is called anthropomorphism.

- Think about the plot of your fable. What is going to happen? Fables are usually quite short. Their purpose is to make the reader think and to teach a lesson, not to be entertaining, like other sorts of stories that you have learned to write.

- The setting and the appearance of the characters is not usually important. Unless the readers need to know about details like that, do not include them in your fable. Concentrate on the story and how it teaches the reader a lesson.

The Highwayman

Here is the beginning of a long poem by Alfred Noyes, which tells the story of a highwayman.

The wind was a torrent of darkness among the gusty trees,
The moon was a ghostly galleon tossed upon cloudy seas,
The road was a ribbon of moonlight over the purple moor,
And the highwayman came riding –
    Riding – riding –
The highwayman came riding, up to the old inn-door.

He'd a French cocked-hat on his forehead, a bunch of lace at his chin,
A coat of claret velvet, and breeches of brown doe-skin;
They fitted with never a wrinkle: his boots were up to the thigh!
And he rode with a jewelled twinkle,
    His pistol butts a-twinkle,
His rapier hilt a-twinkle, under the jewelled sky.

Over the cobbles he clattered and clashed in the dark inn-yard,
And he tapped with his whip on the shutters, but all was locked and barred;
He whistled a tune to the window, and who should be waiting there
But the landlord's black-eyed daughter,
    Bess, the landlord's daughter,
Plaiting a dark red love-knot into her long black hair.

GLOSSARY
brand piece of burning wood
harry annoy, attack
ostler person who looks after horses at an inn
wicket gate or door

And dark in the old inn-yard a stable-wicket creaked
Where Tim the ostler listened; his face was white and peaked;
His eyes were hollows of madness, his hair like mouldy hay,
But he loved the landlord's daughter,
    The landlord's red-lipped daughter;
Dumb as a dog he listened, and he heard the robber say —

'One kiss, my bonny sweetheart, I'm after a prize to-night,
But I shall be back with the yellow gold before the morning light;
Yet, if they press me sharply, and harry me through the day,
Then look for me by moonlight,
    Watch for me by moonlight,
I'll come to thee by moonlight, though hell should bar the way.'

He rose upright in the stirrups; he scarce could reach her hand,
But she loosened her hair i' the casement! His face burnt like a brand
As the black cascade of perfume came tumbling over his breast;
And he kissed its waves in the moonlight,
    (Oh, sweet black waves in the moonlight!)
Then he tugged at his reins in the moonlight, and galloped away to the West.

He did not come in the dawning; he did not come at noon;
And out o' the tawny sunset, before the rise o' the moon,
When the road was a gypsy's ribbon, looping the purple moor,
A red-coat troop came marching —
    Marching — marching —
King George's men came marching, up to the old inn-door.

They said no word to the landlord, they drank his ale instead,
But they gagged his daughter and bound her to the foot of her narrow bed;
Two of them knelt at her casement, with muskets at their side!
There was death at every window;
    And hell at one dark window;
For Bess could see, through her casement, the road that *he* would ride.

Comprehension

A 1   In your own words, describe how the highwayman was dressed.
2   Why was the highwayman coming to the inn?
3   Who was listening to the highwayman talking to the landlord's daughter?
4   Who came to the inn at sunset?
5   What did they do?

B 1   Why do you think the sky is described as 'jewelled' in verse 2?
2   Where do you think the highwayman was going to get 'yellow gold' from?
3   What do you think the red-coats were going to do?
4   Why do you think the poet writes 'There was death at every window'?
5   Why do you think the soldiers gagged and tied up the landlord's daughter?

C   In your own words, tell the story of the highwayman so far.

Vocabulary

Metaphors and similes

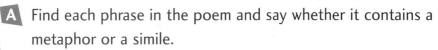

Metaphors, like similes, are expressions that make descriptions more vivid for the reader. A **simile** describes something by comparing it to something else, and usually begins with 'as' or 'like'. For example:

His hair <u>like</u> mouldy hay.

Metaphors suggest similarities between very different things, but don't use 'as' or 'like'. For example:

The moon was a ghostly galleon.

A Find each phrase in the poem and say whether it contains a metaphor or a simile.

1 The wind was a torrent of darkness
2 Dumb as a dog he listened
3 The road was a ribbon of moonlight
4 the jewelled sky
5 His face burnt like a brand

B 1 Look again at the metaphors in part A and write what each means.
2 Think about three or more things in your classroom or outside that you could describe in vivid terms using metaphors. Write down some examples.

Spelling

Adding suffixes

Remember, to add a **suffix** to a word that ends with a consonant, you need to look at the letter <u>before</u> the last letter.

If it is a consonant, or has another vowel in front of it, just add the suffix. For example:

> jump + 'ed' = jumped
> broad + 'est' = broadest

But if it is a vowel, double the last letter before adding the suffix. For example:

> big + 'er' = bigger
> stop + 'ing' = stopping

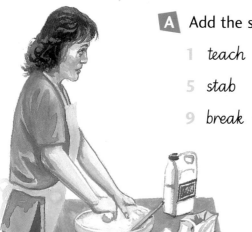

A Add the suffix 'ing' to each word.

1 teach	2 hug	3 turn	4 get
5 stab	6 clap	7 hit	8 drop
9 break	10 gloat	11 skip	12 grab

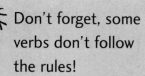
Don't forget, some verbs don't follow the rules!

B Write the past tense of each word.

1 play	2 snap	3 slam	4 trim
5 throw	6 float	7 skim	8 fit
9 bat	10 drip	11 shop	12 hum

Grammar

Noun and verb agreement

When we say nouns and verbs must **agree**, we mean that, in a sentence, the nouns and verbs must match. We usually need different forms of a verb to go with plural nouns and singular nouns.

We use 'is' or 'was' if we are writing about one person or thing. For example:

The **road** <u>was</u> a ribbon of moonlight.

The **poem** <u>is</u> sad.

We use 'are' or 'were' with 'you', or if we are writing about more than one person or thing. For example:

"**You** <u>were</u> lucky they didn't see you" said the man.

The **villagers** <u>are</u> scared of highwaymen.

A Copy these sentences, adding 'is', 'are', 'was' or 'were' in each gap.

1 The sky _____ very clear last night.

2 The stars _____ shining brightly.

3 You _____ looking at them with your telescope.

4 It _____ cloudy tonight.

5 There _____ a full moon.

6 My sister and I _____ too tired to stay up last night.

7 We _____ going to stay up late tonight, instead.

8 "You _____ not staying up after midnight!" Mum said.

B Copy these sentences, choosing the correct verb to complete each one.

1 I <u>like/likes</u> looking at the stars.

2 My sister and I <u>share/shares</u> a telescope Grandad gave us.

3 He <u>know/knows</u> a lot about the stars.

4 We <u>listen/listens</u> when he <u>tell/tells</u> us about the stars.

5 I <u>have/has</u> a book about the stars.

6 Mum <u>say/says</u> she will buy us another book tomorrow.

Remember, we usually add 's' or 'es' to make a **noun plural**, but we usually add 's' or 'es' to make a **verb singular**.

Sentence construction

Pronouns

Remember, **pronouns** are used in place of nouns. For example:
> Bess was the landlord's daughter. <u>She</u> had long black hair.

<u>She</u> stands in the place of <u>Bess</u>.

Possessive pronouns show who or what owns something. For example:
> The ribbon was <u>hers</u>.

<u>Hers</u> stands in the place of <u>Bess's</u>.

Possessive pronouns that describe nouns, for example '<u>her</u> hair', can also be called **possessive adjectives**.

A 1 Copy each sentence, changing the blue nouns into pronouns.

   a   *The highwayman* mounted *his* black horse.

   b   *The horse* galloped away.

   c   *Bess* watched *the highwayman* leave.

   d   *The red-coats* marched down the road.

2 Copy the pronouns from the box and draw a circle around the possessive pronouns.

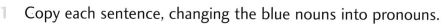

its	*I*	*hers*	*we*	*mine*	*he*	*she*	*his*	*theirs*	*them*	*they*

B 1 Write two sentences about the highwayman, using at least one possessive pronoun in each.

2 Copy each sentence, replacing the blue words with possessive pronouns.

   a   *My brother* said *my brother's torch* was more powerful than *my torch*.

   b   My umbrella has broken, can I borrow *your umbrella*?

   c   The boys packed up *the boys' tent* and helped us with *our tent*

   d   Is that tent *your tent*?

Writing

Narrative poetry

'The Highwayman' is a **narrative poem**. A narrative poem tells a story. 'The Highwayman' tells a tragic story but not all narrative poetry is sad. Narrative poems can be funny, exciting or mysterious.

Just like an ordinary story, every narrative poem has:

- a plot
- a setting
- characters.

1 Read 'The Highwayman' again. How do you think the poem ends? Make some notes on:

- The plot – What might happen in the rest of the poem? Does the highwayman get away? Do the soldiers catch him? Does the landlord's daughter escape from the soldiers and save the highwayman?
- The setting – Will the setting for the rest of the poem be the inn or will you need to describe another setting, for example, if the highwayman escapes and has to hide somewhere?
- The characters – The highwayman, the soldiers, Tim (the ostler), the landlord and Bess have already been mentioned in the poem. Will all of them be in the ending you write? Will you add any new characters?

2 Use your notes to write the end of the poem.

The Man from Snowy River

This poem was written by the Australian poet A B 'Banjo' Paterson (1864–1941).

There was movement at the station, for the word had passed around
    That the colt from old Regret had got away,
And had joined the wild bush horses – he was worth a thousand pound,
    So all the cracks had gathered to the fray.
All the tried and noted riders from the stations near and far
    Had mustered at the homestead overnight,
For the bushmen love hard riding where the wild bush horses are,
    And the stock-horse snuffs the battle with delight.

There was Harrison, who made his pile when Pardon won the cup,
    The old man with his hair as white as snow;
But few could ride beside him when his blood was fairly up –
    He would go wherever horse and man could go.
And Clancy of the Overflow came down to lend a hand,
    No better horseman ever held the reins;
For never horse could throw him while the saddle-girths would stand –
    He learnt to ride while droving on the plains.

And one was there, a stripling on a small and weedy beast;
    He was something like a racehorse undersized,
With a touch of Timor pony – three parts thoroughbred at least –
    And such as are by mountain horsemen prized.
He was hard and tough and wiry – just the sort that won't say die –
    There was courage in his quick impatient tread;
And he bore the badge of gameness in his bright and fiery eye,
    And the proud and lofty carriage of his head.

But still so slight and weedy, one would doubt his power to stay,
    And the old man said, 'That horse will never do
For a long and tiring gallop – lad, you'd better stop away,
    Those hills are far too rough for such as you.'
So he waited, sad and wistful – only Clancy stood his friend –
    'I think we ought to let him come,' he said;
'I warrant he'll be with us when he's wanted at the end,
    For both his horse and he are mountain bred.'

'He hails from Snowy River, up by Kosciusko's side,
    Where the hills are twice as steep and twice as rough;
Where a horse's hoofs strike firelight from the flint stones every stride,
    The man that holds his own is good enough.
And the Snowy River riders on the mountains make their home,
    Where the river runs those giant hills between;
I have seen full many horsemen since I first commenced to roam,
    But nowhere yet such horsemen have I seen.'

So he went; they found the horses by the big mimosa clump,
    They raced away towards the mountain's brow,
And the old man gave his orders, 'Boys, go at them from the jump,
    No use to try for fancy riding now.
And, Clancy, you must wheel them, try and wheel them to the right.
    Ride boldly, lad, and never fear the spills,
For never yet was rider that could keep the mob in sight,
    If once they gain the shelter of those hills.'

So Clancy rode to wheel them – he was racing on the wing
    Where the best and boldest riders take their place,
And he raced his stock-horse past them, and he made the ranges ring
    With the stockwhip, as he met them face to face.
Then they halted for a moment, while he swung the dreaded lash,
    But they saw their well-loved mountain full in view,
And they charged beneath the stockwhip with a sharp and sudden dash,
    And off into the mountain scrub they flew.

Then fast the horsemen followed, where the gorges deep and black
    Resounded to the thunder of their tread,
And the stockwhips woke the echoes, and they fiercely answered back
    From cliffs and crags that beetled overhead.
And upward, ever upward, the wild horses held their way,
    Where mountain ash and kurrajong grew wide;
And the old man muttered fiercely, 'We may bid the mob good day,
    No man can hold them down the other side.'

When they reached the mountain's summit, even Clancy took a pull –
    It well might make the boldest hold their breath;
The wild hop scrub grew thickly, and the hidden ground was full
    Of wombat holes, and any slip was death.
But the man from Snowy River let the pony have his head,
    And he swung his stockwhip round and gave a cheer,
And he raced him down the mountain like a torrent down its bed,
    While the others stood and watched in very fear.

He sent the flint stones flying, but the pony kept his feet,
    He cleared the fallen timber in his stride,
And the man from Snowy River never shifted in his seat –
    It was grand to see that mountain horseman ride.
Through the stringy barks and saplings, on the rough and broken ground,
    Down the hillside at a racing pace he went;
And he never drew the bridle till he landed safe and sound
    At the bottom of that terrible descent.

He was right among the horses as they climbed the farther hill,
    And the watchers on the mountain, standing mute,
Saw him ply the stockwhip fiercely; he was right among them still,
    As he raced across the clearing in pursuit.
Then they lost him for a moment, where two mountain gullies met
    In the ranges – but a final glimpse reveals
On a dim and distant hillside the wild horses racing yet,
    With the man from Snowy River at their heels.

And he ran them single-handed till their sides were white with foam;
    He followed like a bloodhound on their track,
Till they halted, cowed and beaten; then he turned their heads for home,
    And alone and unassisted brought them back.
But his hardy mountain pony he could scarcely raise a trot,
    He was blood from hip to shoulder from the spur;
But his pluck was still undaunted, and his courage fiery hot,
    For never yet was mountain horse a cur.

And down by Kosciusko, where the pine-clad ridges raise
   Their torn and rugged battlements on high,
Where the air is clear as crystal, and the white stars fairly blaze
   At midnight in the cold and frosty sky,
And where around the Overflow the reed-beds sweep and sway
   To the breezes, and the rolling plains are wide,
The Man from Snowy River is a household word today,
   And the stockmen tell the story of his ride.

GLOSSARY

beetled overhung
droving herding or driving animals
stripling young man

Comprehension

A 1 Why had 'all the tried and noted riders' gathered at the homestead?
  2 'No better horseman ever held the reins' is said of which character?
  3 Why did the old man tell the man from Snowy River to 'stop away'?
  4 Where did they find the wild bush horses?
  5 Where did all the riders, except the man from Snowy River, give up the chase?
  6 Why do you think that the riders were anxious to get the colt back?

B 1 Write in your own words what you think the following words mean.
    a cracks (verse 1)   b fray (verse 1)   c mustered (verse 1)
    d resounded (verse 8) e cowed (verse 12)   f cur (verse 12)
  2 Write down the similes in the poem that describe:
    a Harrison's hair
    b how the man from Snowy River raced down the mountain
    c how he followed the wild bush horses.
  3 Explain the following phrases in your own words:
    a made his pile   b doubt his power to stay   c stood his friend
    d took a pull   e standing mute   f a household word

C 1 Make a list of the characters in the poem, with notes on what you know about them.
  2 Describe the setting of the poem.
  3 In your own words, write a summary of the story told by the poem.

Vocabulary

Antonyms in expressions

Remember, **antonyms** are words that have opposite meanings.
Some common **expressions** use antonyms. For example:

All the tried and noted riders from the stations <u>near and far</u>.

A Write an antonym for each word.

1	hot	2	dead	3	cruel	4	love	5	rise
6	dark	7	empty	8	fast	9	rich	10	out

B Use each of these expressions in a sentence of your own.

1 *coming and going*   2 *black and white*

3 *more or less*   4 *through thick and thin*

5 *ups and downs*   6 *take the rough with the smooth*

Spelling

Rhyming words

'The Man from Snowy River' has strong **rhyme**. Some of the rhymes have the same letter patterns, others are different patterns that make the same sound. For example:

And Clancy of the Overflow came down to lend a <u>hand</u>,
No better horseman ever held the <u>reins</u>;
For never horse could throw him while the saddle-girths would <u>stand</u> –
He learnt to ride while droving on the <u>plains</u>.

'Hand' and 'stand' have the same letter pattern.
'Reins' and 'plains' have different letter patterns which sound the same.

A Write down all the pairs of rhyming words from the poem in which the two words have different letter patterns.

B For each of the following pairs of rhyming words from the poem, add two more words that rhyme and have the same letter pattern. The first one has been done to help you.

1 *beast*   *least*   *feast*   *east*

2 *friend*   *end*   3 *place*   *face*

4 *tread*   *overhead*   5 *ground*   *sound*

6 *sway*   *today*   7 *track*   *back*

Grammar

Double negatives

Remember, **double negatives** – two negative words in one sentence – can cancel each other out. The negative sentence becomes positive. For example:

No use for no fancy riding now.

A Correct each of these sentences, so that they are negative and mean what the writer really intended. Underline the changes you have made.

1 There wasn't nothing they could do to catch the horses.

2 There isn't no chance that colt is fit for a long, hard gallop.

3 I haven't seen nothing half as good as that young horse.

4 He didn't never slow down.

B Write in your book whether the word 'anything' or 'nothing' should be added to each of these sentences.

1 He realised there wasn't _____ he could do if the pony fell.

2 There was _____ for it but to hold on tightly.

3 The onlookers could do _____ but stand and watch.

4 Couldn't they do _____ to help?

Punctuation

Pauses

In the poem on pages 60–63 there are various punctuation marks to show where the poet wants the reader to **pause**. For example:

> But still so slight and weedy, one would doubt his power to stay,
> And the old man said, 'That horse will never do
> For a long and tiring gallop – lad, you'd better stop away,
> Those hills are far too rough for such as you.'
> So he waited, sad and wistful – only Clancy stood his friend –
> 'I think we ought to let him come,' he said;
> 'I warrant he'll be with us when he's wanted at the end,
> For both his horse and he are mountain bred.'

A 1 Neatly copy the verse above and circle the punctuation marks that are used for pauses.

2 Write a few sentences about the different punctuation marks you circled in question 1 and the length of pause you think each one stands for.

B 1 Look again at the poem on pages 60–63. Copy other lines from the poem that contain examples of each type of punctuation mark you found in part A.

2 Write some sentences of your own, using each type of punctuation mark that indicates a pause.

Writing

Ballads

Remember, a **narrative poem** tells a story. A **ballad** is a form of narrative poetry. Ballads have existed for hundreds of years.

The first ballads were not written down but passed by word of mouth from generation to generation, telling stories of exciting adventures and brave deeds. They were often sung to simple tunes. Ballads often had a rhyming pattern in which the first and third lines rhymed and the second and fourth lines rhymed. In the sixteenth century, ballads were written down and sold at fairs and on street corners.

A Write another verse for 'The Man from Snowy River', to go between the last two verses.

- Think about the plot. What might happen when the man from Snowy River returns with the horses?
- Think about the setting. Will this verse take place where the other riders stopped or will they meet the man from Snowy River back at the homestead?
- Think about the characters. You probably don't need any new characters but you could describe how Clancy, Harrison and the others react when the man from Snowy River comes back with the horses.

You should have 8 lines in your verse. These lines should have the following rhyming pattern:

- lines 1 and 3 rhyme
- lines 2 and 4 rhyme
- lines 5 and 7 rhyme
- lines 6 and 8 rhyme.

B Write a ballad of your own about one of the following:

- a cat rescued from a tree
- a football match
- a boat surviving a terrible storm.

Anansi

There are lots of traditional Caribbean stories about Anansi, the spider. Here is part of a Jamaican story about Anansi and Kling Kling, a bird. Anansi and Kling Kling have had an argument.

For a long time Anansi tried to catch Kling Kling. They were friends no longer. Anansi set traps and hid them in the grass near the berries on which Kling Kling loved to feed. He made the withes from the woods into long, slippery nooses and hid them where Kling Kling liked to walk. But it was no use. Kling Kling was too clever. He saw all the traps and avoided them. Sometimes he would hide in the top of a tree and, without a sound, watch Anansi set a trap. Then when it was all done he would suddenly cry out "Why?" and fly away, leaving Anansi puzzled and angry.

At last Anansi went to his friend, Tiger, and said:

"I beg you, Mr Tiger, help me to catch that old Kling Kling bird. He flew away, and I cannot catch him at all."

GLOSSARY
Br'er brother
withes flexible twigs

"And what will you give me if I help you catch him?" asked Tiger.

"Oh, my sweet Tiger," said Anansi, "I will give you a cow."

"A whole cow?" asked Tiger, who was very greedy and very fond of cow.

"A whole cow, Mr Tiger. I promise," said Anansi. So Tiger thought and thought for a long time and at last he said, "I tell you what we will do, Br'er Anansi. I will lie down in the house and pretend to be dead. You must take a bell and walk all round the town calling out at the top of your voice, 'The great King Tiger is dead; the great King Tiger is dead.' Then all the people will come to the funeral, and you can catch him."

Now the next day was a great market day. Kling Kling went to the market and bought peas and rice and codfish and plantain and sweet potatoes. While he was buying the sweet potatoes he heard a bell ringing, and he asked the people what it was. "Ah," said a stout market-woman, "the great King Tiger is dead."

"What! You mean that Tiger, the great Tiger, is dead?" asked Kling Kling.

"Yes," said the people standing round. "Yes, what she says is true. The great King Tiger is dead."

"And when did he die?" asked Kling Kling.

"Yesterday just before twelve o'clock."

"Then," cried Kling Kling, "I must hurry away to put on my second-best coat and go to the funeral." Kling Kling rushed home and put on his second-best two-tailed blue coat and his shoes that were so new that they cried out "quee-quee" when he walked in them. When he had finished dressing Kling Kling went to Tiger's house. When he got there he saw a great crowd of people outside, and he shook his head and said, "So the great King Tiger is dead!"

"Yes," they replied. "The great King Tiger is dead."

"When did he die?"

"Yesterday, just before twelve," they replied.

"What killed him? Was it fever? Was it an accident? How did he die?"

"The heat of the weather killed him," they said.

"And has he laughed at all since he died?" asked Kling Kling. "No."

"Then he isn't dead at all," said Kling Kling. "Don't you know that a man is not dead until he laughs a big last laugh?"

Tiger was in the nearest room, listening at the window. When he heard what Kling Kling said he broke out into a great laugh that shook the house, and Kling Kling said, "Ha-ha, I never yet heard a dead man laugh!" and he flew away. So Tiger never got the cow.

from *Anansi the Spider Man* by Philip M. Sherlock

 ## Comprehension

A
1 What did Kling Kling like to eat?
2 How did Anansi try to catch the bird?
3 What reward did Anansi offer Tiger for catching Kling Kling?
4 What was Kling Kling buying when he heard a bell ringing?
5 How did Kling Kling guess that Tiger was not dead?

B
1 Do you think Tiger's plan for catching Kling Kling was a good one? Give reasons for your answer.
2 Do you think Tiger was wise or foolish? Why?
3 Do you think Kling Kling was wise or foolish? Why?

C
1 Is this story written in the first person or the third person?
2 If Kling Kling told the story, which of these would he not know:
   * that Anansi was trying to catch him
   * that Anansi offered Tiger a cow in exchange for his help
   * that Tiger was not really dead.
3 If Tiger told the story, which of these would he not know:
   * that Kling Kling watched Anansi setting traps
   * that Anansi was trying to catch Kling Kling
   * that Kling Kling came to the funeral.

Vocabulary

Using a thesaurus

A **thesaurus** is very useful for finding words to use when you are writing descriptions. It can help you choose the most suitable word to use, and lists synonyms, so you can avoid repeating words.

A 1 Look up the following words in your thesaurus. Write down all the synonyms for each word.

a friend   b fright   c journey
d map   e push   f sudden

2 Choose one synonym for each word in question 1 and use it in a sentence of your own.

You might need to alter some sentences slightly.

B Improve these sentences by finding better words or phrases to replace those in pink type. Use a thesaurus to help you.

1 Anansi *asked* Tiger to help him.

2 Anansi *got cross* when he could not *get* Kling Kling.

3 Tiger thought of a *good* plan.

4 Kling Kling *got the idea* that Tiger wasn't really dead.

Spelling

Adding suffixes

This rule doesn't apply to adding 'ing'.

There are special rules for adding most **suffixes** to words that end with 'y'. If the 'y' sounds like 'ee', as in 'fr<u>ee</u>', we usually change the 'y' to an 'i' before adding the suffix. For example:

ugly (sounds like 'ugl<u>ee</u>'), so ugly + 'ness' = ugl<u>i</u>ness

A Add the suffix 'ness', 'ment' or 'ly' to each word.

1 heavy   2 haughty   3 merry   4 funny

5 naughty   6 silly   7 pretty   8 nasty

B Write the root word and the suffix in each of the following words. The first one has been done to help you.

1 carried   carry + 'ed'

2 lazily   3 daintiness   4 happily   5 paid

6 tidiness   7 wearily   8 glorious   9 loneliness

Grammar

Prepositions

Prepositions are words that tell us where something is – its position. For example:

    below   around   on   under

A Write down the preposition from each sentence.

1 Kling Kling went to the market.

2 Kling Kling hid in the tree.

3 He flew above the trees.

4 He saw a crowd beside Tiger's house.

A **prepositional phrase** is a group of words that tells you the position of something. It usually begins with a preposition, ends with a noun or pronoun and doesn't contain a verb. For example:

    Tiger was <u>in the room</u>.

B Write a sentence using each of the prepositional phrases below. Underline the prepositions in your sentences.

1 on the branch   2 near the bush   3 under the bridge

4 by the house   5 in the grass   6 behind the door

Punctuation

Practising
punctuation

A Copy this passage, adding the missing capital letters, commas and full stops.

jamaica an island in the west indies is the third-largest island in the caribbean sea located south of the island of cuba and west of the island of hispaniola jamaica is about 235 km long and is 82 km at its widest point highlands running from east to west cover a large proportion of the island the highest part of jamaica is in the blue mountains to the east jamaica's main crops are sugar tropical fruits coffee and cacao which are grown for sale both in jamaica and to other countries

B Rewrite this conversation, adding the capital letters, speech marks and other missing punctuation, and starting a new line when each new person speaks.

did you know that christopher colombus reached jamaica in may 1494 asked the teacher yes i did said the boy my father was telling me about jamaicas history the other day what else did he tell you enquired the teacher he told me that at that time the island was populated by arawak indians replied the boy but these people soon died out and slaves were brought from africa to work in the sugar-cane fields

Writing

First person and third person

Most stories are in either the **first person** or the **third person**.

The third person is used when the person telling the story is not a character in the story. For example:

<u>The girl</u> walked down the street.

The first person is used when the story is written from the viewpoint of one of the characters in the story. For example:

<u>I</u> walked down the street.

The Anansi story on pages 68–70 is written in the third person. The writer, Philip M Sherlock, is not one of the characters in the story. He is writing about other characters. If the story had been written as if it was by one of the characters, the viewpoint would be different. The character writing the story can only write about what he/she knows, heard, saw or did.

A Read the Anansi story again. Now tell the story from Kling Kling's or Tiger's point of view. Remember, you will need to write 'I' and not 'he'. You will also need to think carefully about how much that character would know. For example, Kling Kling would not know that Anansi had offered Tiger a cow in return for catching him.

B 1 Think of another way in which Anansi or Tiger might have tried to catch Kling Kling. Write a few paragraphs about it to add to the story. Use the third person to write the paragraphs.

2 Rewrite the paragraphs you wrote in question 1. This time, write them in the first person, as if you are Kling Kling. Tell only the things that Kling Kling could have known about.

How the Earth Began

Nearly every culture has ancient stories about how the Earth was created. These stories were told to satisfy people's curiosity about their planet. The stories are usually about a powerful god who creates the Earth. Below are two stories about the creation of the Earth, from two different cultures.

The Bible Story of Creation

In the beginning, everything was dark. There was no world at all, only emptiness, but God was there and he was not dark or empty.

God said, "Let there be light!" And there was light. Now life could begin.

So God shaped the world; he made the sky, the land and the sea. The Earth was hot. Fire rumbled in the heart of the mountains. They exploded. Then, slowly, the Earth cooled, leaving rich soil where plants could grow. God was pleased with the world he had made.

Now he wanted plants to grow on the Earth. Green shoots

sprang up, and flowers opened their bright petals. Grass spread over the hills and valleys and a gentle wind rustled the leaves of countless trees. God saw that it was all good.

The green shoots grew tall and yellow. Grain ripened in the sun, but no little harvest mice ran through the corn. No birds nested in the tall trees. No children played yet in the new world.

So God spoke to the sea and the sky, "Be filled with living things, too!" Fish of every shape and colour filled the sea. In the sky above, birds flew, soaring high as they sang. Insects hovered over the Earth. Then God said, "Let the Earth be filled with animals of every kind!" Large animals roamed over the Earth, and small ones scuttled after them. The air was filled with roars, neighs and squeals. God blessed the animals. Their numbers grew. God was pleased with everything he had made.

Now the Earth was ready for people to live on it. God took a handful of soil and made a man. He breathed his life-giving breath into him. The man was different from all the other animals God made.

The Ancient Egyptian Story of Creation

In the beginning, before there was any land and Egypt did not exist, all was darkness, and there was nothing but a great waste of water called Nu. The power of Nu was such that there rose out of the darkness a great shining egg, and this was Ra.

Now Ra was all powerful, and he could take many forms. His power and the secret of it lay in his hidden name; but if he spoke other names, that which he named came into being. "I am Khepera at the dawn, and Ra at noon and Turn in the evening," he said. And the sun rose and passed across the sky, and set for the first time.

Then he named Shu, and the first winds blew; he named Refnut the spitter and the first rain fell. Next he named Geb, and the Earth came into being; he named the goddess Nut, and she was the sky arched over the Earth with her feet on one horizon and her hands on the other. He named Hapi, and the great River Nile flowed through Egypt and made it fruitful.

After this, Ra named all things that are upon the Earth, and they grew. Last of all, he named humankind, and there were men and women in the land of Egypt.

Then Ra took on the shape of a man and became the first Pharaoh, ruling over the whole country for thousands and thousands of years, and giving such harvests that for ever afterwards the Egyptians spoke of the good things that happened 'in the time of Ra'.

 **Comprehension**

A Look at 'The Bible Story of Creation' on pages 76–77.

1 What was the Earth like when God first created it?
2 How did God feel about the world he had made?
3 What was God's command when he created fish, insects and birds?
4 From what did God make the first man?
5 How did he make the man come to life?

B Look at 'The Ancient Egyptian Story of Creation'.

1 Where did Ra come from?
2 Of what was Refnut the god?
3 What goddess became the sky?
4 What is the great river that flows through Egypt?
5 What did Ra do after he had created men and women?

C In many ways, the Bible story of creation and the Egyptian story of creation are similar but, in some ways, they are different. Answer the following questions to compare the two stories.

1 Who was responsible for creation in each story?

2 How were the creators different?

3 How did the creators make things in each story?

4 Make a list of all the things created in the Bible story and the order in which they were created.

5 Make a list of all the things created in the Egyptian story and the order in which they were created.

6 Look at your answers to questions 4 and 5. Are there any similarities? Are there any differences?

Vocabulary

Alphabetical order

Remember, to put a group of words into **alphabetical order**, you need to look at the first letter of each word. If they start with the same letter, you need to look at the second letters. If the second letters are the same, you need to look at the third letters, and so on. For example:

bible   countless   coward   creation   crept   crest   crib

A Write each set of words in alphabetical order.

1 bread   birth   before   badge   blind   bundle

2 crew   force   carry   fast   courage   feast

3 power   water   rain   praise   wind   river

4 neutral   needle   neither   never   neglect   neighbour

B Check whether each set of words is in correct alphabetical order. Write whether each set is 'correct' or 'incorrect'. Write each incorrect set of words in correct alphabetical order.

1 strain   straight   stranger   strangle   stretch   strap

2 remain   remember   reminder   remote   relic   relative

3 practise   perfect   price   probe   prune   pry

4 pretend   prevent   proper   propose   prospect   prosper

Our Planet   unit **10**

Spelling

Using a dictionary

A Use your dictionary to check the spelling of each word below. Write whether each is 'correct' or 'incorrect'. Write the correct spelling of each incorrectly spelled word.

1 ripen	**2** godess	**3** decieve	**4** handfull
5 afterwards	**6** religion	**7** diferent	**8** controll

B Seeing letter patterns within words helps you to develop your dictionary skills and spelling. Each of the following words contains a number of shorter words. See how many you can find. The first one has been started to help you.

1 landscape   *land   and*

2 understandable   **3** sometimes

4 therein   **5** consideration

Grammar

Writing for your audience

When you write, it is important to make sure that your writing will suit your **audience** (the people who will be reading it). If you are writing for younger children, you need to use simple words and short sentences.

A Rewrite each of these sentences in a simpler style, so it would be easier for young children to understand.

1 Green shoots sprang up, and flowers opened their bright petals.

2 Grass spread over the hills and valleys and a gentle wind rustled the leaves of countless trees.

3 In the beginning, before there was any land of Egypt, all was darkness, and there was nothing but a great waste of water.

B For each word below, write a word or phrase that means the same but would be easier for a young child to understand. Use your dictionary or thesaurus to help you.

1 feast	**2** countless	**3** create	**4** jovial
5 transform	**6** reveal	**7** ancient	**8** courageous

Sentence construction

Clauses

Remember, a **clause** is a group of related words that includes at least one verb, and is part of a sentence. For example, this sentence has two clauses:

Green shoots sprang up, and flowers opened their bright petals.

| clause 1 | clause 2 |

Sentences with only one verb have only one clause. For example, this clause is also a sentence:

God was satisfied.

The **main clause** in a sentence can stand on its own as a complete sentence. For example:

The Earth was hot and there were no living things.

'The Earth was hot' is the main clause. It could also be a sentence on its own.

Don't forget the auxiliary verbs!

A Copy these sentences. Underline the clause or clauses in each. Circle the verb or verbs in each clause.

1 Large animals roamed over the Earth and small ones scuttled after them.

2 No birds nested in the tall trees.

3 Now Ra was all powerful, and he could take many forms.

4 The sun rose and passed across the sky, and set for the first time.

5 Last of all, he named humankind, and there were men and women in the land of Egypt.

B Look through another book and find some long sentences. Copy two or three, and underline the clauses and circle the verbs in each.

Writing

Reviewing text

When you are asked to write a **review** of something you have read, you need to:

- briefly describe it
- express your opinion
- give reasons for your opinion.

If you are asked to compare two pieces of writing and say which you prefer, you need to:

- briefly describe the two pieces of writing
- express your preference
- give reasons for your preference.

A Read again 'The Bible Story of Creation', and write three paragraphs:

- paragraph 1 – a brief summary of the story
- paragraph 2 – your opinion of the story – Did you like or dislike it? Did you find it easy or difficult to read?
- paragraph 3 – reasons for your opinion.

B Read again 'The Ancient Egyptian Story of Creation', and compare it to the Bible story. Write three paragraphs:

- paragraph 1 – a brief summary of what the stories are about
- paragraph 2 – your preference (which story you preferred)
- paragraph 3 – reasons for your preference.

The Giant of Grabbist

Just behind Dunster, a village in Somerset, is a steep hill called Grabbist. The legend of the Giant of Grabbist, below, has been written down just as it was told by an old man from the village, who remembered being told the story when he was a boy.

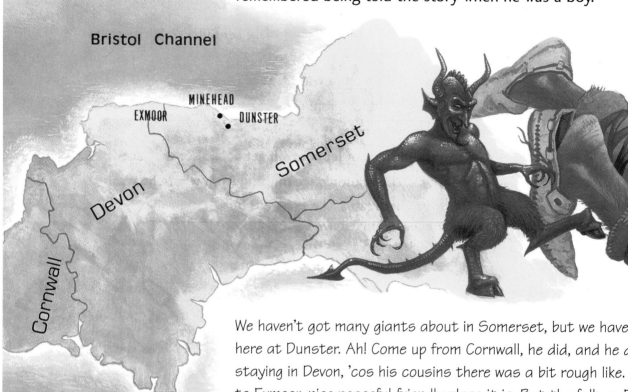

Bristol Channel

MINEHEAD

EXMOOR · DUNSTER

Somerset

Devon

Cornwall

We haven't got many giants about in Somerset, but we have one down here at Dunster. Ah! Come up from Cornwall, he did, and he didn't like staying in Devon, 'cos his cousins there was a bit rough like. He come up to Exmoor, nice peaceful friendly place it is. But the folk on Exmoor, they didn't like the size of him. Bit scared they was. But then they found out he didn't harm anyone. They got quite fond of him. And then farmers' wives they began to put their heads together. "What does the poor great fellow feed on?"

Well, I think they were ready to cook a dinner for him, but they found they needn't. You see, he was fond of fish. He did wade out down channel right out to sea, and all the fishing boats had to do was to follow him. Oh! They come into Minehead harbour loaded, they did. He'd go and wade out there, and water come up to his armpits, and he'd scoop up great shoals o'fish, and 'twas a wonderful time for the fishing boats.

Well now, one time old Elijah Crowcombe in the leaky old *Dorcas Jane* was loaded right up and she was a-wallowing in the waves when a storm comes up. Well, they thought they was a-going down, when through the storm the giant comes a-striding, and he picks up *Dorcas Jane*, and afore they could say "Thank you", he puts her down quiet and safe like in Watchet harbour.

Well now, Giant he was very happy on Exmoor, and then the Old Nick came back 'cos he didn't like seeing the little thatched churches going up all over the way. So when the folk of Hawkridge thought they'd build themselves a church, and Giant would help them, Old Nicky didn't like it. Ah! So when Giant was coming by Spire Cross with a load of great stones, Old Nicky tripped him, and stones went all abroad.

Well, Giant didn't say nothing, he didn't lose his temper as Old Nicky hoped he would, and cause a storm. No, he just patiently bent, and he picked them up one after another, and he put them up on Hawkridge for the church. And a great broken one he tossed into the very wood where the Old Boy was sat chuckling, and that made him go off in a hurry. And the rest of the stones, that weren't no good for churches, he laid them across the river Barle, and made Tarr Steps.

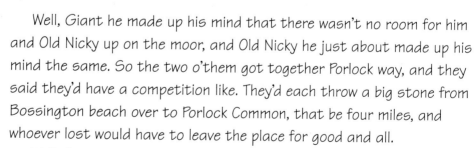

Well, Giant he made up his mind that there wasn't no room for him and Old Nicky up on the moor, and Old Nicky he just about made up his mind the same. So the two o'them got together Porlock way, and they said they'd have a competition like. They'd each throw a big stone from Bossington beach over to Porlock Common, that be four miles, and whoever lost would have to leave the place for good and all.

Well, Old Nick had first throw, and his stone it flew out over four miles and it landed up on Porlock Common. And then Old Nick he trips up Giant, and his stone fell only three feet away. But Giant didn't go away. No, he just trips Old Nick himself and sat right down on him for a rest, while Old Nick squirmed underneath. After a while, the Giant picks up Old Nick by his tail, and he said, "That weren't a fair throw. We'll throw from Quantock later on. Meanwhile, you go cool your head." And he tossed Old Nick right out down channel, out over Porlock Bay.

Giant picked up his stone and throwed right over to Battlegore, six mile away! "Your turn now," he says. Old Nicky was dancing with rage, and I think he was so cross about it, that his stone fell down, and the giant's was the furthest off. "Now," says the giant, " 'tis your promise to go away from here, and never come back no more. But as no one can trust you, I'll make sure." And he picked up Old Nicky by his tail, and he waded out down the Severn Channel, till he was right out to sea, 'twas up to his armpits. And then he gave him a good swing three times round his head, and let go. Well, I reckon the Old 'Un landed about the West Indies!

Comprehension

A Copy these sentences, filling in the missing words.

1 _____ is a steep hill behind Dunster.

2 At first, people were frightened of the giant, then they realised he didn't _____ anyone.

3 The giant liked to eat _____.

4 Old Nicky and the giant had a _____ to see which of them would stay, and which would go.

B Write sentences to answer these questions.

1 What evidence did the villagers have that the giant was kind?

2 Who do you think Old Nick/Old Nicky/the Old 'Un was?

3 What evidence can you find in the story to show that the giant was very calm and in control when dealing with Old Nicky?

C Is this story written:
- like most other stories you have read?
- as if the story-teller is speaking to you?
  Give reasons for your answer, quoting words and phrases from the story.

 Vocabulary

Dialect

In different areas of the country, people may pronounce some words differently when they speak. This is known as a regional **accent** or **brogue**. In most areas, people use some words or phrases that are only used in that area. This is called **dialect**. People from other areas sometimes find it difficult to understand regional accents and dialect.

A Try to work out what these people are saying. Write down each person's speech and your 'translation'.

B Make a list of phrases from your part of the country that outsiders might have difficulty in understanding.

87

Spelling

'gue' letter pattern

The passage on pages 84–86 is a record of the old man's **monologue**. A monologue is a long speech by one person.

'Monologue' is pronounced 'mon-oh-log' because it has a silent 'u' (we don't pronounce it).

The '**gue**' letter pattern with a silent 'u' occurs at the end of a number of words. For example:

prolog<u>ue</u> (means 'an introduction at the beginning of a book or play')
brog<u>ue</u> (means 'a strong shoe' and also 'a regional accent')

A Write down the answers to the following clues.

1   weariness   *f a _ _ g u e*

2   not clear   *v _ g u e*

3   a Jewish place of worship   *s y n _ _ _ g u e*

4   somebody who is up to no good   *r _ g u e*

5   conversation   *d i _ _ _ g u e*

B Use a dictionary to find the definitions of the 'gue' words below. Write down your answers.

1   catalogue   2   vogue   3   league   4   intrigue

Grammar

Standard English

When we write, we usually use English as carefully and correctly as possible. This is called **Standard English**. When we speak, we don't usually use Standard English quite so carefully. The legend on pages 84–86 has been written down just as the old man said it, in his Somerset dialect. The story is interesting, but the grammar is sometimes not standard.

A Copy the phrases and sentences below, changing the purple words into Standard English.

1 They thought they **was a-going** down.

2 He **puts** her down **quiet** and **safe**.

3 They **come** into Minehead harbour.

4 where the Old Boy was **sat** chuckling

5 he **gived** him a good swing

6 "That **weren't** a fair throw,"

7 there **wasn't no** room

8 He **throwed** it over to Battlegore, six **mile** away.

B Write a Standard English phrase or sentence to replace each of these informal, spoken ones.

1 Come up from Cornwall, he did

2 'cos his cousins there was a bit rough like

3 and stones went all abroad

4 afore they could say "Thank you"

5 the two of them got together Porlock way

6 they said they'd have a competition like

7 whoever lost would have to leave the place for good and all

Sentence construction

Conjunctions

Remember, **conjunctions** are joining words. Sometimes we use them in pairs. For example:

The giant was <u>both</u> kind <u>and</u> helpful to the villagers.

Other pairs of conjunctions include:

either	or
neither	nor
whether	or
not only	but also

The conjunctions always go immediately before the words they join. For example:

The giant was <u>neither</u> prepared to live with Old Nicky <u>nor</u> move away.

A Use different pairs of conjunctions to fill the gaps in these sentences.

1 In the story, the devil is called _____ 'Old Nick' _____ 'the Old Boy'.

2 Some villagers couldn't decide _____ the giant should stay _____ go.

3 The giant had lived _____ in Somerset _____ in Cornwall.

4 Old Nicky was _____ kind _____ helpful to the villagers.

B Write a sentence of your own using each pair of conjunctions.

1 either   or

2 not only   but also

3 neither   nor

Writing

A writer's style

When we talk about **a writer's style**, we mean how a writer:

- constructs sentences – some writers use long, complicated sentences, others use short ones
- chooses vocabulary – some writers use common, everyday language in a 'chatty' style, others may use more formal language.

The style of a piece of writing must suit the audience. A children's story written in long, complicated sentences with lots of difficult words would not be much good!

The style of 'The Giant of Grabbist' is chatty, written as if the story-teller is actually speaking to you. It is written in a Somerset dialect.

A Choose one paragraph from 'The Giant of Grabbist' and rewrite it in a style that is more like the stories you are used to reading. For example:

> Well now, Giant he was very happy on Exmoor, and then the Old Nick came back 'cos he didn't like seeing the little thatched churches going up all over the way.

> Giant was very happy on Exmoor, but Old Nick returned because he didn't like seeing the little thatched churches being built everywhere.

B Imagine that Old Nick did not get thrown all the way to the 'West Indies' but came back and tried to get the better of the giant again. Write the story about what happens. Write in the same chatty style as 'The Giant of Grabbist', just as if you were talking to your reader.

Poems About Strange Beasts

The Dragon of Death

In a faraway, faraway forest
lies a treasure of infinite worth,
but guarding it closely forever
looms a being as old as the earth.

Its body is big as a boulder
and armoured with shimmering scales,
even the mountaintops tremble
when it thrashes its seven great tails.

Its eyes tell a story of terror,
they gleam with an angry red flame
as it timelessly watches its riches,
and the dragon of death is its name.

Its teeth are far sharper than daggers,
they can tear hardest metal to shreds.
It has seven mouths filled with these weapons,
for its neck swells to seven great heads.

Each head is as fierce as the other,
Each head breathes a fiery breath,
and any it touches must perish,
set ablaze by the dragon of death.

All who have foolishly stumbled
on the dragon of death's golden cache
remain evermore in that forest,
nothing left of their bodies but ash.

by Jack Prelutsky

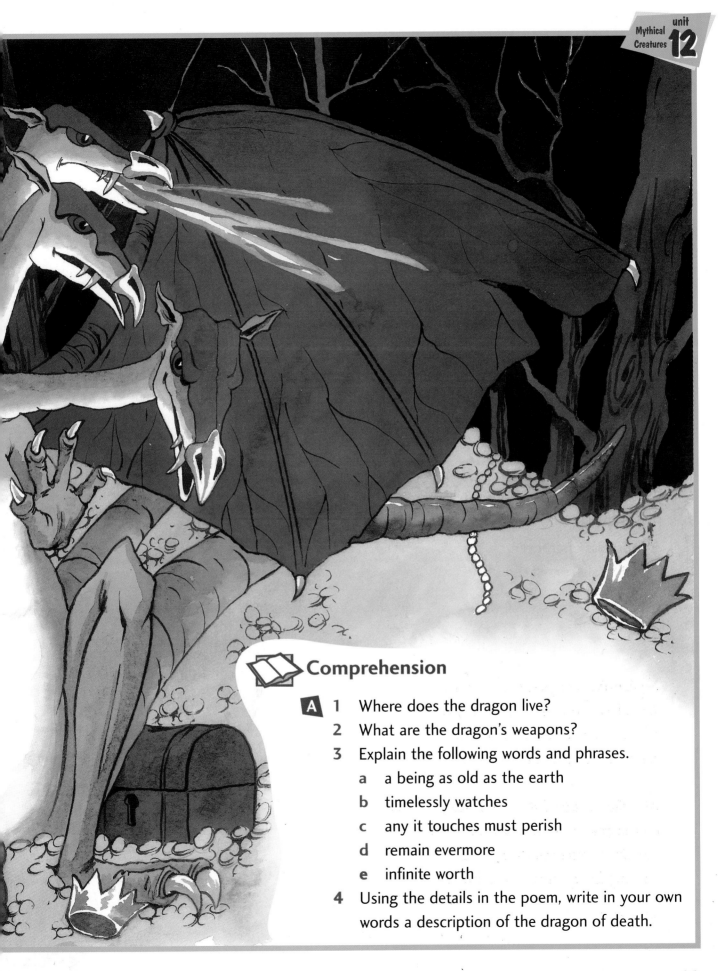

Comprehension

A 1 Where does the dragon live?

2 What are the dragon's weapons?

3 Explain the following words and phrases.

a a being as old as the earth

b timelessly watches

c any it touches must perish

d remain evermore

e infinite worth

4 Using the details in the poem, write in your own words a description of the dragon of death.

Anancy

Anancy is a spider;
Anancy is a man;
Anancy's West Indian
And West African.

Sometimes, he wears a
    waistcoat;
Sometimes, he carries a cane;
Sometimes, he sports a top hat;
Sometimes, he's just plain,
Ordinary, black, hairy spider.

Anancy is vastly cunning,
Tremendously greedy,
Excessively charming,
Hopelessly dishonest,
Warmly loving,
Firmly confident,
Fiercely wild,
A fabulous character,
Completely out of our mind
And out of his, too.

Anancy is a master planner,
A great user
Of other people's plans;
He pockets everybody's food,
Shelter, land, money, and more;
He achieves mountains of things,
Like stolen flour dumplings;
He deceives millions of people,
Even the man in the moon;
And he solves all the mysteries
On earth, in air, under sea.

And always, Anancy changes
from a spider into a man
And from a man into a spider
And back again
At the drop of a sleepy eyelid.

by Andrew Salkey

 **Comprehension**

B 1 What do you think the first two lines of the poem mean?

2 How do you think Anancy can be both West Indian and West African?

3 What do you understand by 'vastly cunning'?

4 Explain what the poet means when he says that Anancy is:
'Completely out of our mind
And out of his, too.'

C Write a paragraph to explain whether you prefer 'The Dragon of Death' or 'Anancy'.

Vocabulary

Using a dictionary and a thesaurus

A Use your dictionary to find the meanings of these words from the two poems.

1 looms ('The Dragon of Death' verse 1)
2 armoured ('The Dragon of Death' verse 2)
3 ablaze ('The Dragon of Death' verse 5)
4 cache ('The Dragon of Death' verse 6)
5 sports ('Anancy' verse 2)
6 vastly ('Anancy' verse 3)

B Use a thesaurus to find some other words the poet could have used to describe the dragon of death. For example:

- its body
- its breath
- its scales
- its head
- its eyes
- the treasure.

Spelling

Adjectives and adverbs

If a word describes a noun, it is an **adjective** and if it describes a verb, it is an **adverb**.

Remember, if a word can be changed by adding 'er' or 'est', or has 'more', 'most', 'less' or 'least' in front of it, then it is probably an **adjective** or **adverb**. For example:

Adjective: Its teeth are far <u>sharper</u> than daggers
Adverb: It roared <u>more fiercely</u> than before

A Make the comparative and superlative of each word. The first one has been done to help you.

1 hard   *harder   hardest*

2 strong   3 fast   4 intelligent

5 terrible   6 fierce   7 heavy

B Copy the sentences below. Underline and label each adjective and adverb and draw a circle around the noun or verb it describes.

1 He could run faster than the rest of us.
2 The room was the coldest in the house.
3 I shouted more loudly to attract their attention.
4 That was the most boring film I have ever seen!

Grammar

Word classes

The four most important **word classes** (parts of speech) are:

- **nouns** – naming words
- **adjectives** – describe nouns
- **verbs** – action or being words
- **adverbs** – describe verbs.

You have learnt that many words can be altered by adding or taking away **prefixes** and **suffixes**. Some words can be made into all four parts of speech. For example:

Noun: enjoy<u>ment</u>
Adjective: enjoy<u>able</u>
Verb: enjoy
Adverb: enjoy<u>ably</u>

A Copy and complete the table below. Use your dictionary to check all the spellings and that you have each part of speech correct.

Noun	Adjective	Verb	Adverb
playfulness			
	reliable		
irritation			
		agree	
			boastfully
			satisfactorily
		amaze	
	sympathetic		

B Copy the green words from each sentence and write down whether each is a noun, an adjective, a verb or an adverb.

1 I accidentally dropped Graham's radio.
2 It fell with a terrible crash.
3 I realised with horror that it was broken.
4 Graham stormed in angrily.
5 In a loud voice, he asked what I had done.
6 I confessed that I had been careless.

Punctuation

Apostrophes for possession

Remember, to show that something belongs to someone or something, add an **apostrophe** and an 's' to make the noun into a **possessive noun**. For example:

The dragon's treasure was very valuable.

dragon is a noun

dragon's is a possessive noun

A Write each phrase in a shorter way, using a possessive noun. The first one has been done to help you.

1 the tail of the cat   *the cat's tail*
2 the teddy belonging to the baby
3 the eyes of the dragon
4 the crown of the king
5 the hat belonging to Anancy
6 the cover of the book
7 the birthday of Maria
8 the ladder belonging to the woman

Remember, plural nouns usually end in 's'. To make them possessive, add an apostrophe after the 's'. For example:

I entered the three dragons' den.

For nouns that are plural, but don't end with 's', we add an apostrophe and an 's'. For example:

The mice's cheese.

B 1 Make each of these plural nouns into a plural possessive noun by adding an apostrophe in the correct place.

a *girls*   b *dogs*   c *childrens*

d *schools*   e *books*   f *womens*

2 Write a sentence using two of the possessive nouns you wrote in question 1.

Mythical Creatures **unit 12**

98

Writing

Performance poetry

The two poems you have read are both about mythical creatures but they are very different in form and style.

'The Dragon of Death' has six four-line verses, with lines 2 and 4 rhyming in each verse. 'Anancy' has five verses of different lengths, and some rhyme while others don't.

'Anancy' is a **performance poem**. That means it is meant to be read aloud by one or more people. A performance poem can be performed in many different ways. For instance, the first four lines of 'Anancy', which have a very steady rhythm, could be chanted by one group in between all the other verses as well as at the beginning.

A Read the poem 'Anancy' again, and make notes on how you would perform it. You should decide:
  • How many people would perform the poem?
  • Which lines each person/group of people would say?
  • How the lines would be said – for example, chanting, loudly, quietly, quickly, slowly, getting louder and faster, etc.

B Make up a mythical creature of your own about which you can write a performance poem. First, make notes on what the creature looks like and what it does. Then write the poem, following the pattern of 'Anancy':

Verse 1 – explain what the creature is
Verse 2 – describe what the creature looks like
Verses 3 and 4 – describe how the creature behaves
Verse 5 – finish the poem with a verse that sums up the creature.

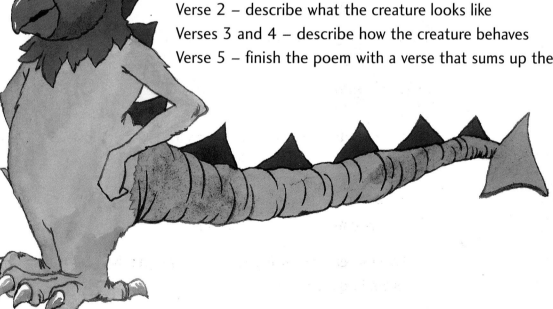

Check-up

 Vocabulary

A Copy and complete each **idiom**, then write in your own words what it means.

1 to go behind someone's _____
2 to lend a _____
3 to find your _____
4 to take the lion's _____

B Make a word web for each of the words below, adding as many words as possible from the same **word family**.

1 believe
2 happy
3 contented
4 arrange

C 1 Rewrite the following sentence five times, each time using a different **synonym** for 'said'.

"May I come in?" said Mike.

2 Copy your answers to question 1, adding a different adverb to each, for example:

"May I come in?" enquired Mike courteously.

D Use a **prefix** to make the **antonym** of each word.

1 complete
2 afraid
3 probable
4 tolerant
5 loyal
6 frequent
7 like
8 responsible

E Write whether each sentence contains a **metaphor** or a **simile**.

1 The sun's rays were golden arrows.
2 The music sounded like a babbling brook.
3 His face was a mask of fury.
4 My hands were as cold as ice.

F Write each set of words in **alphabetical order**.

1 hound   hostage   hostile   hospital   hostel
2 screen   scrub   scream   scribble   scrape

Spelling

A Choose and copy the correct spelling of each word below.

1 *exeption*   *exception*   2 *excpect*   *expect*

3 *extreme*   *exctreme*   4 *excamine*   *examine*

5 *exact*   *excact*   6 *excitement*   *exitement*

B Add the **suffix** to each word.

1 *smile + 'ing'*   2 *confuse + 'ion'*   3 *believe + 'able'*

4 *hate + 'ful'*   5 *hope + 'less'*   6 *relate + 'ion'*

C Write a **homophone** for each word.

1 scent   2 pain   3 meet   4 new

5 rain   6 knight   7 pair   8 steel

D Write the **past tense** of each verb.

1 *slim*   2 *show*   3 *sit*   4 *slap*

5 *trip*   6 *sell*   7 *swim*   8 *drag*

E For each word below, write three words that **rhyme** and have the same **letter pattern**.

1 heather   2 bright   3 pace   4 cream

F Add the **suffix** 'ness', 'ous' or 'ly' to each word.

1 *ugly*   2 *guilty*   3 *mystery*   4 *busy*

5 *empty*   6 *angry*   7 *fury*   8 *fussy*

G Make the **comparative** and **superlative** of each word.

1 *tight*   2 *wide*   3 *unpleasant*   4 *smooth*

5 *certain*   6 *urgent*   7 *funny*   8 *lonely*

Grammar

A Copy and complete each sentence, choosing the correct **verb** to fill the gap.

1 Bill *is/are* painting the wall.

2 Mum and Dad *was/were* visiting Grandad.

3 Cleo *is/are* feeding the ducks.

4 The windows *is/are* dirty!

5 The weather *was/were* very cold.

6 The dogs *was/were* tied up outside the shop.

B Copy a long sentence from any passage in this book. How many different ways can you rearrange the words and phrases? You may change one or two of the smaller words if you need to. Each of your sentences should make sense.

C 1 Write a short conversation using **direct speech**.

2 Rewrite the conversation your wrote in question 1, using **reported speech**.

D 1 Make a list of five **common nouns**.

2 Make a list of five **proper nouns**.

E Copy and correct each of these sentences, so that it means what the writer intended.

1 I'm not never going to finish this!

2 He won't do nothing to help me.

3 There's not no way we'll catch that bus.

F Use each of these **prepositional phrases** in a sentence of your own.

1 around the corner   2 under the table   3 behind the door

G Write an **adjective**, a **verb** and an **adverb** that can be made from each of the following nouns.

1 irritation   2 playfulness   3 satisfaction   4 annoyance

Punctuation and sentence construction

A Write each of these sentences twice, first in the **past tense** and then in the **future tense**.

1   I am helping my father.

2   They are cleaning the windows.

B Copy each sentence below. Draw a line under the **subject** of each sentence and draw a circle around the **verb**.

1   The children searched in the shed.

2   The shed was very cluttered.

3   Sally asked Paula to help her.

4   They lifted some heavy tools.

C 1   Write the following passage as **direct speech**.

Rory asked if he could borrow my ruler. I said that I could not find it. He enquired when I had last seen it. I replied that the last time I remembered having it was when I had lent it to him the day before.

2   Add some sentences of your own to complete the conversation.

D Write a short **recount** in the past tense, describing something you had to do in the last few days that you would have preferred not to have done.

E Expand each of the following sentences by adding another **clause** or two to make it more interesting.

1   The stray dog ran towards us.

2   I grabbed its collar.

3   We took it to the police station.

4   The dog looked sad.

F Copy each sentence below, using a **possessive pronoun** in place of the words in colour.

1   My bike had a puncture, so my sister lent me her bike.

2   I haven't got a pen. May I use your pen?

3   That pizza is the pizza belonging to them. This pizza is the pizza belonging to us.

G Copy this conversation, starting a new line when necessary, and adding all the missing **capital letters and punctuation**.

did you know how far scarborough was before we left I asked dad yes but i didnt realise *that there would be so much traffic he replied i expect its because its august bank holiday dont you yes i agreed wishing we were on the beach not stuck in a hot car*

H Copy each sentence, underlining the **clause** or clauses. Draw a circle around each **verb**.

1 *I opened the window and looked out.* 2 *It was a beautiful day.*

3 *Trying not to make a noise, I crept downstairs.* 4 *I went into the garden.*

I Use each pair of **conjunctions** in a sentence of your own.

1 *not only but also* 2 *either or* 3 *whether or*

J Make each of these plural nouns into **possessive nouns** by adding an **apostrophe** in the correct place.

1 *dogs* 2 *children* 3 *cars* 4 *teams* 5 *women* 6 *players*

Writing

Look at the story starting point below. Choose one of the writing tasks to do.

Write the opening for a story based on the starting point. Make a quick draft of the plot but, when you write your story, begin in the middle of the plot. Remember, you will need to think of a way to tell the reader what has already happened.

Make brief notes on plot, setting and characters for a playscript based on this starting point. Write the first scene, remembering to include the setting, characters' names, dialogue and stage directions.

Use the starting point as the basis of a legend. Remember, legends usually include brave deeds, heroes and heroines, and often feature gods and goddesses.

Story starting point:
A Daring Escape

Make some notes on the characters you would have in a story based on this starting point. Choose two of the characters and write a conversation between them which lets the reader know what these characters are like.

Plan and write a narrative poem based on the starting point. Remember, you will need to think about plot, setting and characters.